Set Up

KARL BECKER

SET UP TO WIN

THREE FRAMEWORKS TO A HIGH-PERFORMING SALES ORGANIZATION

First Printing 2021
ISBN 978-0-578-84962-1

Improving Sales Performance
improvingsalesperformance.com

To everyone committed to improving themselves,
their teams, and their companies

Contents

Introduction:
The Big Play

Building Systems That Help You Achieve Win After Win

Right now, you might feel like your company just can't catch a break. Maybe there's one thing you're missing—something under your nose that, if you could just pinpoint it, would hold the key to creating stable and predictable revenue and achieving your revenue goals. If only the stars would align and shine their light on that singular, magic solution.

For over twenty-five years, I've worked with leaders of companies who have burnt themselves out trying tactic after tactic to revive sales. They want off the hamster wheel of chasing the latest sales and marketing trends, and they know they need to do something different… but what? Fortunately, I've seen most of these leaders experience not one but multiple aha moments—when all the elements they needed to achieve and increase revenue move into alignment. These moments come when people stop focusing on individual tactics and start widening their scope.

It's possible. I know it is.

Alignment comes when a leader looks beyond the money they make and the leads they're bringing in. Things start clicking as they come to understand their company's foundations, their customers, and perhaps most importantly of all, the people in their sales organization. I've seen individual performance rise and confidence grow in both team members and those managing them as they all come together and feel valued. I've seen the health of sales cultures improve with a positive correlation to the revenue a company brings in. I've seen stressed-out leaders relax and move themselves out of roles they don't want and into roles they love, focused on their highest and best-use activities.

Coming into alignment is a key to succeeding in life—inside business and outside of it. When you bring that alignment together with intentionality, your results can almost seem magical. But here's the catch. That one magical thing that makes everything fall into place only does so after you've purposefully set the stage and put in the work.

Here's an example. It starts with a trip to a Rockies baseball game in 2013 and ends with a system I developed to repeat something that might seem like pure luck.

I'd gotten two free club-level tickets from a friend who couldn't make it to the game, and I decided to bring my seven-year-old son Sam along.

When I told him what we were doing that night, he was thrilled. He also immediately jumped to "We're gonna catch a ball tonight!"

"Yeah," I said, "we sure are!" We jumped up and down laughing and enjoying the ridiculousness of our idea. We were going to be out late, and having a mission like this was definitely going to make it more fun for both of us.

We were already in the car when my son said, "Dad! We forgot the gloves!" I waited while he ran back into the house to get them. Then, all the way to the game, he kept repeating the mantra, "We're gonna catch one! We're gonna catch one!"

When we reached our seats, Sam started to pantomime catching balls out of the air. I started doing the same, his energy was so contagious.

"We're gonna catch one! We're gonna catch one!"

By then, I was dead set on catching a ball for my son. But of course, as we continued to hype each other up, I had some fleeting anxiety.

What if this really happened, and I became the dad who accidentally knocked his kid over, and the Jumbotron footage got played on an ESPN blooper reel over and over? I shook the thought out of my head and focused.

We're gonna catch one.

That year, Rockies player Michael Cuddyer had won the 2013 National Batting League Title. When he came up to bat, I thought, *How about now?*

As if by magic, Cuddyer hit the ball straight toward me. I stood up, put my glove up, and caught the ball perfectly. Then I handed it to Sam.

And do you know what he said?

"Dad, when are we going to catch the next one?"

Back home we celebrated and shared our prize with my wife and younger son, Morgan. I knew that I now needed to get a ball for him too.

How could I make this win happen again? How would one make a process out of getting a baseball at a major league game?

First, you bring kids, because baseball players love to throw balls to kids. That's why I take my family to a lot of baseball games. When we go to one in a different city, we usually buy hats and shirts with the home team's logo, and we choose seats where we're most likely to catch a ball. Then, you do everything you can to focus on the game and hold the intention that you're going to catch that ball. And of course, don't forget to bring your glove! After all, chance favors the prepared.

When the whole family went to a Texas Rangers game, it was time to test the process. We'd bought our Rangers gear, and as we sat there, I started repeating to myself: *I'm going to catch a ball today. I'm going to catch a ball today.*

I had zero doubt at that moment, but as the innings went by, there was still no ball.

Then the game went into an extra inning. At last, a pop fly from the Mariners bounced off some nearby bricks and rolled back into the field. The third baseman for the Rangers, Adrián Beltré (three All-Star nods, three Gold Glove Awards, two Silver Slugger Awards and four-time

Rangers Player of the Year, no less), picked it up and looked around. He saw me sitting with Morgan and tossed the ball to us.

What if we'd had Mariners shirts on instead of Rangers? What if I wasn't with my kid, and instead somebody who was with their kids sat next to me? What if we hadn't sat behind third base? Would I have gotten the ball?

Probably not.

Now, all told, we have gone to seven stadiums and have collected five balls. (It would have just been four, but we caught two at a Kansas City Royals game on Memorial Day the year after they won the World Series—a ball for each of my kids that night!)

It was the alignment of all these different elements that created the conditions most likely for me to be able to get a baseball and give it to my son. It's true that I could have gone to that Rangers game and not walked out with a ball. And that has happened. But if I would have been there day in and day out, following that same pattern, eventually it would have worked. I can hold the proof in my hands.

I wasn't satisfied just catching the one ball, and you're not going to be satisfied with landing one successful customer or making one sale, no matter how great it is. To be able to replicate your success, you're going to have to change a lot of little things.

You can't just say, "I got our new marketing agency," or, "I increased my pricing," or, "I hired this really great sales guy." Doing just one of these things is not creating success.

In this book, I'm going to show you how to put together the Three Frameworks that will help you create an environment where luck can find you: the Revenue Equation, the Individual Performance Planner, and the Revenue Planner. You'll be unlocking the strengths of each of your individual players, and as a leader, you'll get more clarity and certainty about what the rules of the game are and how you can prepare your team to catch the ball when it comes their way.

Through a process of open communication, active listening, reflection, and collaboration, I've been able to bring teams together not only to build stronger organizations but to improve the performance, and overall happiness, of individual salespeople. I've systematized it and learned to replicate it, and in the following pages, I'm going to show you how to do it yourself to serve your own organization.

If you're struggling with revenue to the point that you need an immediate win, please first read chapter 9. It'll give you some tips that might help you achieve some revenue stability within three months, and you can do them before making any major systemic changes. If, after reading that chapter, you're able to pick out a couple of things to get your revenue as stable as you can, I encourage you to do so. After all—Sam and I did get that first baseball before developing the system that would allow us to catch more in the future.

Be aware, though: finding a quick win won't erase the problems that are holding your business back from achieving the revenue that you want and need. You'll soon reach another ceiling, and it may not be that much higher than where you are now.

A shot of adrenaline now might bring you back from the brink of disaster, but it won't heal your business's underlying problems. Putting in the time and attention is what's going to do it, whether or not you go for a quick win first. I recommend you return to chapter 1 and work through the Three Frameworks that I lay out for you to achieve stability and long-term growth. This will establish a series of small wins that each build on the one before. The frameworks I've created are meant to help you create systems and processes that stabilize your revenue, a thorough approach to enriching the lives and work of your salespeople, and a plan for making the most of the revenue currently available. Anything you do to enhance revenue after working through these frameworks will be that much more effective.

Chapter 1:
What Is Holding You Back?

Factors That Keep Companies from Achieving Stable Revenue

If you've picked up this book, you're probably looking for ways to grow your sales, build a healthier sales organization, get predictable revenue, decrease your business stress, and rebalance your life. Whether it's some or all of these things, you most likely have seen mini wins but nothing sustainable. The things you've tried so far aren't working, and even if they have here and there in the past, you're beginning to feel like those successes might have just been luck.

You want to grow your business into something stable. You want to be intentional about your sales tactics and bring them to life without having to completely start from scratch every time. You want your salespeople to be on message as they represent your company, to be an extension of your brand, to be successful month in and month out, and even to enjoy themselves at work! And when you're feeling especially optimistic, you might daydream about being able to accurately predict your short-term *and* long-term revenue, increase your net income, and have a clear and certain path to hitting your revenue goals.

Instead, right now, you might have salespeople who frustrate you. Maybe you feel they need to be more organized, have better attention to detail, be more proactive, and follow up more. You might even see them leaving early every day even as they complain they don't have enough leads.

Maybe you have tried all the usual tactics to bring in new customers (SEO, paid search, ads, social, lead magnets, webinars, email blasts—you name it!) and still you find yourself with erratic and inconsistent revenue each month. Or maybe you find that the only way to boost revenue is to provide big discounts and promotion after promotion to incentivize sales.

Whatever your sales symptoms might be, you are over it and you want change. You want things to get simpler, more predictable, and more stable.

Strong foundations and sustainable success aren't just for big corporations. It's possible for small- and medium-size businesses (SMBs) and start-ups to create systems that keep sales moving steadily upwards, all while keeping your company morale high and your culture healthy.

I know it's possible because I've seen it happen again and again. For over twenty-five years, I've worked with companies and individuals on navigating change, building sales organizations, and developing high-performing teams. Those experiences have helped me develop the Three Frameworks that, when completed, make successful sales sustainable and repeatable.

To get you in the headspace to learn about this, there's a major myth that we need to smash first. It's one I've heard over and over from leaders and sales teams at almost every company I've worked with.

The Myth of the Miracle Cure

Popular culture has tricked people into thinking that if there is some-thing wrong with our lives, there's one single reason why it's happening. Books and movies talk about someone's big "tragic flaw" that leads to their downfall. Hamlet was indecisive. Darth Vader couldn't control his anger. Achilles had that Achilles' heel.

In the same way, advertisements can lead us to believe that there is one solution that will chase away each of our problems. Low energy?

Drink this health tonic. Dry skin? Use this lotion. Hate where you're living? Move to this new housing development.

You even see this kind of oversimplification in sports. The Chicago Cubs didn't win a World Series for seventy-one years, and many sports fans, famously a superstitious bunch, blamed this losing streak on the Curse of the Billy Goat, which a local character named William Sianis cast when he wasn't allowed to bring his pet goat in to the fourth game of the 1945 World Series.

You probably have heard this part of the story, but what you might not know is the following. In October of 2016, the Cubs hosted a fundraiser for the animal rights group Farm Sanctuary, with the tongue-in-cheek purpose of reversing the Curse of the Billy Goat. Two weeks later, they won the World Series.

I'm going to go out on a limb here and say that the reason the Cubs didn't win the series for seventy-one years was not because of William Sianis and his goat. I also don't think it was because the equipment they had wasn't good enough or because the team somehow managed to get a batch of poor players every single year. Thinking that one of these things was holding the Cubs back from winning shows a common fallacy: that a single magical unicorn—or in this case, goat—holds the key to all your problems.

No matter how much we look for a miracle cure, our problems are never caused by just one thing, and they can't be solved by just one thing either.

But when it comes to a stalled-out sales organization, leaders almost always start by incorrectly blaming a lack of leads for their inability to grow.

Salespeople, Order Takers, and Identity Crises

United Events is an event production company that manages audio-visual and technical production for advertising agencies, corporations, associations, and nonprofits. When another company has an event they are planning, United Events is there with the equipment and skills to bring those events to life. They called me to help them bring in more revenue by finding them more leads. What I actually found was that the number of leads was the least of their problems.

Before this engagement, I had built lead generation engines for many companies. What got me excited to work with United Events was that all their leads 100 percent needed the services they sold. After all, how could you hold an event if you didn't have the audiovisual gear and a team to make sure your message could be seen and heard by your audience?

So, I came up with an approach to identify and prospect leads by finding out what events were coming to their area. The logic was simple: fish where the fish were by identifying and then contacting the organizations that had upcoming events.

As was my normal practice, I started by making a list of people coming to their area in the near future to hold events. Before calling and emailing event organizers, I brought a question to United Events' CEO, Mark.

"Why do people buy from you?" My plan was to use his answer to open up conversations with these potential customers.

Mark told me that one major competitor was the in-house audio-visual teams at hotels where these events often took place. Typically, the hotel would charge their in-house events companies a 50 percent commission for any leads that came through the hotel to the audio-visual company, so they'd have to charge a higher price to pay for the commission and also ensure they could make a profit.

"We can save these leads coming to these hotels at least 20–25 percent versus the in-house company because we don't have to pay that commission to the hotel," Mark said.

That's what I went with when my team contacted each person on our newly formed lead list. When people responded that they were interested, my team immediately distributed those leads to United Events' salespeople to follow up.

About a month and a half later, the salespeople responded to me. "Karl, we can't sell based on price," they said. "The in-house company's prices are always better, and we can't beat them."

This was news to me, and it told me that nobody really knew what made United Events different from the competition. The leads weren't bad—they just didn't understand what was truly being offered to them. Nobody at United Events seemed to understand, so how could these potential customers?

However, as I said before, the problem is never caused by just one thing. There was also a major problem with how the leads were being handled, which is what I discovered when I started interacting more closely with Tyrone, one of the salespeople.

My team had just sent Tyrone an introduction to Laura, an event planner who was coming to town and had shown interest in United Events after my team emailed her. "She wants to talk to you. Could you reach out and set an appointment with her to talk about her event and introduce her further to the company?"

A couple of days later, I'd heard nothing back.

"I've been too busy to get to it," Tyrone said when I checked in with him. "Can you just send me their RFP? That's all I really need."

I was dumbfounded. "When you ask for a request for proposals," I said, "that tells the event planner that you're thinking about this as a commodity and that you're selling on price. But we already know that doesn't work, right?"

"No, it's just that once I get the RFP, then I can talk to her about it," he said.

I'd revealed another major problem with the way their sales organization was conducting business. Most of the salespeople thought all the leads we brought in were basically sold on United Events already and were just being delivered to them to close the deal. They were leapfrogging over all the work of getting to know the customer's unique situation, what they needed to consider and evaluate, and what they needed to de-risk their decision.

Essentially, they'd reduced the salesperson role to that of someone just providing a quote and then taking an order. Now, on top of not knowing what made their company different from the rest, the salespeople at United Events also weren't meeting the customers on their levels, to then guide them to the point of buying. At that point, I realized that we needed to go back to go forward and unveil all of the many problems that were contributing to the company's struggle to sustain and grow.

Who This Book Is For

If you are a one-person operation that sells monkeys to zoos, this book probably isn't for you. If you're the CEO of Google, it probably isn't for you either.

If you're looking for a meteoric rise in revenue so you can sell your company in two years and split, you might not want to build the sustainable company I'm talking about here. And if you don't really care about leading a happy group of people who grow together as a team, this book is definitely not for you.

If you are a leader of an SMB with five to fifty employees, and if your people's well-being matters to you, you'll 100 percent get something out of this, and so will your team!

I've worked with family businesses, founder-led companies, venture-backed start-ups, companies that sell products, companies that sell experiences…and pretty much everything in between. Each started from a different point of origin before I began to work with them, and the leaders have shown a number of different characteristics that you might find relatable.

Do any of the following situations sound familiar?

The Spaghetti Thrower
WE'VE TRIED EVERYTHING—WHY AREN'T WE GROWING?

Before I arrived, United Events was in a cycle of flinging random solutions at the wall. When I arrived, the sales team looked at me like I was being excluded from an inside joke.

"So, you're Mark's flavor of the month?" Jackie, one of the salespeople, asked me in one of our first meetings. "No offense, but we've done all of these mission statement writing, sales training, marketing, and team development–type things before, and none of it ever really sticks."

Apparently, Mark was the kind of leader who was constantly grasping for new solutions that might increase sales. However, none of the things he tried was the secret sauce that would finally make their spaghetti stick to the wall. The rigamarole was that Mark would try a tactic, thinking that it would finally be the thing that got them on the road to stability and growth. It might be a new CRM (tech for customer relationship management), or an aggressive social media ad buy, or a daylong company team-building retreat. When he didn't see results right away, he'd give up and move on to something else, and so would his team.

Constantly having to change trajectories with no reward was frustrating for Mark. It was also frustrating for his team, who had lost their spark a long time ago. They were so unsure of what they were supposed to be doing, they were operating on autopilot.

When I got there, United Events didn't know who they were and were treating sales as if it were a mechanical process that was malfunctioning. When I was done working with them, they had grown their revenue by $2 million and gone from a group of individual salespeople each doing things their way to a unified team who loved coming in to work and performing their absolute best.

The Cinderella Story
THE CLOCK IS TICKING. WE NEED TO GROW THIS NOW.

Bay Area Games was the quintessential millennial start-up. The two founders, Josh and Rahul, were in their early thirties and had spent the last two years of their lives working on something that wasn't bringing in any revenue whatsoever.

When they hired me, it was right when their work was finally starting to pay off—and it was paying off more than just a little bit. Someone from a seed fund had taken interest in their company and had just put a whole bunch of money into it. The founders hired ten of their friends, who all ate, slept, and breathed Bay Area Games.

Their model was based on a relationship with brand partners who wanted to be seen by gamers and building a gamer base who wanted what those brand partners had to offer. Their idea was great, and now they had the financial validation to run with it. The problem was that they knew they didn't have much time to score those first, most difficult sales. They had found themselves in a chicken-and-egg scenario, with very high stakes for their company.

It was like when you're trying to land your first job: companies only want to hire people with experience, but how will you get experience if no one will hire you? In this case, how could they get enough gamers to impress the brand partners they wanted to keep without having any way to incentivize that gamer base yet?

If they couldn't prove that their idea would sell, they wouldn't get a new round of funding. Like Cinderella at the stroke of midnight, Bay Area Games' carriage would turn into a pumpkin and they'd be back where they'd been before. Being able to make crucial early sales would determine their ability to continue to scale and get another round of funding. They knew if they didn't climb this learning curve quickly, they'd be letting all of their friends, their investors, and themselves down.

With so much on the line, and midnight fast approaching, Josh and Rahul brought me in to help them quickly create offerings and an adaptive sales process that would appeal to different potential brand partners. In true tech start-up style, we designed a series of tests and made small changes according to the responses we got—compressing the sales cycle and decreasing risk by not going big with an untested idea for generating sales.

Using this method, we found out what value we could provide to brand partners and what type of partner liked our solutions the most. We also discovered the best ways to move these customers through the sales funnel and the best key performance indicators (KPIs) to measure our successes as we tested and pivoted. Streamlined weekly sales meetings helped an already highly collaborative group better fly in formation.

The story of Bay Area Games is far from over, but establishing the brand partner program was an early success. We created a replicable sales system that would help them scale, and it kept their carriage from turning into a pumpkin—they scored another round of funding and are still dancing at the ball. And these early wins validated Bay Area Games' value proposition to investors and the picture of success that Josh and Rahul had painted for them.

The Runaway Train
WE BRING IN MONEY, BUT WE'RE ALWAYS IN SURVIVAL MODE.

Online Academy is an online learning company that provides programs for professionals to improve their business skills through workshops, lessons, coaching, and certifications. I was brought in because their director of sales had stepped down, and Dave, their CEO, needed me to train their four salespeople into a better-functioning team.

"We're not having revenue problems," he said to me. "Generally, we book the same number of appointments per month and have a steady close rate of 25–30 percent. If we could just get that close rate up, and maybe get rid of some waste, that would help us reach our goals."

Totally straightforward, or so I thought.

I started looking for places to tighten up the sales funnel and started educating the salespeople on better sales techniques, but not long after that, Dave called me with news that changed my focus.

"Just so you know, we're running our regular end-of-year sale this month," he said. "We're going to discount the hell out of our products and drive revenue as hard as possible, and that should cover our expenses in the next sixty days…including paying you."

He chuckled, but I didn't. I warned him that continuing to run sales like this was going to undermine all the revenue he could be making. What about all the people who were about to buy at full price but then would be going for the discount instead? What about the people who had just purchased at the regular price only to see a sizable discount on the thing they'd just purchased? Having major discounts could also devalue the offering in the minds of potential customers, and in the minds of the salespeople too!

But Dave was adamant that these sales worked every time. They were how Online Academy had consistently made ends meet for years.

So, we worked out a compromise.

"Dave, instead of just discounting, how about we bundle? We offer people a choice of a discounted course or a bundled course with an add-on when they pay full price?" I suggested.

This ended up being a first step toward some major foundational changes in the way Online Academy brought in revenue. While still providing a special offer, we were setting a new precedent for valuing the company's offerings on something other than price. People who received sales and marketing materials from Online Academy now wouldn't just be taking price into consideration when they were evaluating whether to buy or not—they'd be thinking about all the benefits they could get.

We were also making it easier for the salespeople to use the content of the courses and the special add-ons as selling points…instead of the urgency of "This deal is ending soon!"

When the data came back, it showed that a lot of people who bought opted for the bundle instead of the discount. With that, we were on the way to a sea change.

My focus wasn't on snagging a few quick wins here and there to help Online Academy boost revenue. There were foundational ways that the company could tune up their operation, which would make a major difference in how much they were able to earn.

When I started working with them, Online Academy was indeed bringing in consistent revenue. The company was growing, but they didn't know how to manage their growth sustainably. They were de-valuing their offerings because they were only selling them based on price. Every day, they felt like they were on the brink of disaster.

Within nine months of working to fix their sales processes, we multiplied revenue by a factor of 1.5, had increased prices by 20 percent, and had brought up net income by 200 percent.

MAYBE YOU SEE YOUR COMPANY in Online Academy or one of these other companies. Maybe you're stuck in a rut or are constantly anxious about being able to pay everyone on your team, or you're worried that if you don't start growing soon, you'll lose everything.

If any of these problems are familiar, this book is here to help.

The Three Frameworks to a High-Performing Sales Organization

It's natural to want an easy fix, a big win that makes everything fall into place. Real life shows us that this almost never happens, and that's as true in business as it is anywhere else. While a big win here and there is possible, and pretty darn nice when it happens, getting to a place where you're happily humming along usually results from a series of small wins.

It also comes from cooperation and hard work.

Once a leadership team decides they want to put the time and effort into becoming a high-performing sales organization, they bring in someone to act as a Change Agent and lead the group through each step of the process. That's usually the role I play. For you, that role can be filled by an outside consultant, or it can be someone who works in your organization—maybe even you. We'll get into this more in the next chapter.

The Change Agent works with a core group of company staff called the Improvement Team. This team may be made up of salespeople, marketers, and people responsible for business development. If the company is small enough, everyone might be on the Improvement Team. Often it will just be salespeople, with folks from other departments guest-starring here and there when their input is needed.

Over the course of three months to a year, you'll establish the following Three Frameworks to transform your sales organization into something that serves everyone better, from you as the leader, to your sales and marketing people, and to your current and future customers.

Framework #1—The Revenue Equation

The Revenue Equation combines the three factors that, when optimized, create the basis and systems that you will use to guide everything that your organization does. After administering a quick survey called the Revenue Equation Diagnostic to determine how much work needs to be done, it's time for the team to dig in and develop those three factors.

Sales Foundations + Sales Design + Sales Infrastructure = Revenue Stabilization and Growth

SALES FOUNDATIONS: WHO ARE YOU?

These are the values and characteristics that make your business unique. Without knowing your Sales Foundations, which I discuss in chapter 5, without knowing why your company and your offering are unique, you will struggle to sell to others. A lack of proper Sales Foundations was the problem that Mark, United Events CEO, made when he told me to use a 20–25 percent lower price for events as a selling point with the leads my team was emailing and calling.

SALES DESIGN: WHO DO YOU SELL TO?

If you're going to find and sell to the right customers, you need to know who they are and what their current state looks like. Chapter 6

shows you what you need to go past creating ideal customer personas…
to charting out each persona's unique sales journey. If United Events
salesperson Tyrone, for example, had been able to identify where event
planner Laura was on her sales journey instead of just asking for an
RFP, he may have been able to close that sale.

SALES INFRASTRUCTURE: HOW WILL YOU SELL IT?
Now that you know all these things about yourself and your customer,
in chapter 7, you build the processes to act on that information. Map
every team member's responsibilities and all the steps it will take
to move your customer through their sales journey, without leaving
anything out or anyone behind. Online Academy desperately needed
help with their Sales Infrastructure to organize the tens of thousands
of leads that were trapped in their sales funnel.

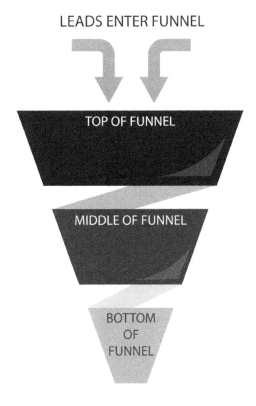

Framework #2—The Individual Performance Planner

Everyone has worked together to create your Revenue Equation. Now, you are going to focus on each individual who will be following those guidelines. Working with each salesperson to discuss their strengths, you can, together, set short- and long-term goals for their lives inside and outside of work and have them create their own Individual Performance Planner. Their intentionality about being their best and your intentionality about supporting them are key if you're going to get the most value out of all the hard work you just did with your Revenue Equation.

Framework #3—The Revenue Planner

Finally, it's time to put everything together to free your trapped revenue, find some quick wins, and accelerate sales and profitability. With your new understanding of your business, customers, funnel, and the people working in your sales organization, you have all the tools to stabilize your sales and get them to trend upward. You'll learn how to use everything you've already put into place and create a plan to achieve quick wins within three months, stabilize your revenue in the following three months, and realize intentional revenue growth in the following twelve months (and beyond).

Who Is at the Center of It All?

Everyone wants revenue growth, but most people gravitate toward crutches or magic bullets instead of digging deep to find the core problems that are preventing them from getting to where they want to go. Time and time again, these methods fail people. It's true that getting clear on your and your customers' identities and getting your systems in order are vital, but everything really depends on the people who make up your sales organization.

In my years working to build companies and sales organizations, what I've found is that everyone wants to foster the kind of environment where people are happy to work. That kind of environment is a natural outgrowth of using this framework. The entire process revolves around how empowered your Improvement Team is and how much trust is built up between its members. When people feel like they're in a safe place, they will be able to honestly point out areas that need to be improved, identify your best customers, and show you what they really have to offer when they're at their best.

Following these Three Frameworks isn't about reaching a specific endpoint. But if you do follow it with intentionality, you will build a healthy company culture and sustainable revenue growth.

Chapter 2:
Who Will Do the Work?

Identifying the Change Agent

So, you've decided to bring your Improvement Team together to complete your company's Revenue Equation, Individual Performance Planner, and Revenue Planner. In that case, you need a particular kind of person to lead this process of discovery, alignment, and implementation. I refer to this person as the Change Agent.

When I say, "Change Agent," what do you think of first?

Some people might think of a motivational speaker who comes into your organization and gets you excited about writing a vision statement and some key differentiators. Maybe they'll throw feel-good buzzwords around, make everyone wear matching T-shirts, and drag you out to a ropes course on a Saturday morning. Other people might break out into a cold sweat, thinking a stranger in a suit and a Rolex is going to kick down the office doors and start berating everyone about how they should "Always Be Closing."

Neither of these is really an accurate picture of someone who brings true and lasting change to a sales organization (especially not that second one). Bringing the Improvement Team into alignment is a multistep process, so the Change Agent needs to have a set of skills to make that alignment happen. In this chapter, I talk about how a Change Agent should interact with the group in a way that brings out all their best qualities. We also review soft skills that the Change

Agent can use to keep things moving while creating a safe place for everyone to be honest and open to new ideas.

Backseat Drivers Welcome!

Recently I went golfing with my older son, Sam, at a course that he had been to before, but I hadn't. As I waited for Sam in the golf cart area, there was a woman maybe ten or fifteen years older than I am, also waiting. She gave me a nod in greeting, and we started making small talk.

"Teaching your son to golf?" she asked when she saw Sam coming toward us from the clubhouse. "My dad used to take me out here when I was around his age."

"Actually, he's the one who wanted to start coming out here," I said and gestured toward my clubs. "I had to dig these out of the garage— and they're not the only things that are a little rusty." We both laughed.

Sam hopped into the cart next to me, and as we were getting ready to take off, I told him, "This is a new course for me, so if you see me doing something wrong or going the wrong way, will you please say something?"

As Sam agreed, the woman said, "Wow! I wish my dad would have told me that. My life would have been so much better if he had."

I'm sure we've all had someone in our lives who always had to be right. Maybe it was a parent, a grandparent, or a teacher who made us feel like we weren't being heard. There's something about being listened to that raises the bar for what you can accomplish, and this woman probably wondered how things may have been different had she felt the freedom to speak her mind around her dad as a kid.

A lot of people experience this feeling of limitation at work when their ideas are ignored or they feel like they might be criticized if they don't toe the company line.

How many more sales organizations would be thriving if they only listened to their people? As Change Agent, when I ask team members to share their opinions, I'm usually met with relief. Most salespeople welcome a clear idea of who they are as a company, who they really want to sell to, and how they should be selling, but a lot of the time they don't get the opportunity to share their questions or ideas.

When you bring in a Change Agent to improve your sales organization, you are not bringing in someone to "whip them into shape." The Change Agent isn't a dictator. They don't send a "my way or the highway" message. The goal is to affect powerful, lasting change in the organization, and in my experience, the only way to bring that about is to be open-minded and to respect everyone's seat at the table.

Without your team's buy-in and honest, thoughtful input, trying to develop your Revenue Equation is pointless. It will just become a new set of rules to follow (or ignore). To make real change happen, and for your Improvement Team to get excited about it, your greatest tool is their brains, eyes, and ears.

For instance, when I'm driving with my family, sometimes I'll say, "I have a blind spot here. If you see something, tell me."

Naturally, there will need to be some ground rules. It's not okay to grab the steering wheel. It's not okay for someone to shout, "Look out!" and throw everyone into a state of panic. I just want them to let me know, "There's a guy on a bicycle rolling up to the stop sign behind us." It's not a big deal. It's just something that will help us all get home successfully.

The Change Agent doesn't become offended when the team lets them know what's up. Just like we're faced with sun glares, blind spots, and distractions when we're driving, it's impossible for the Change Agent to have a perfectly clear view of everything that's going on at all times. The well-being of the sales organization—and all the people who are part of it—is more important than the Change Agent's ego.

That attitude might not usually be the kind you take when you're behind the wheel, but as a Change Agent, I actually want the team to act as backseat drivers. This kind of openness to input is not a natural state for a lot of people, and it might not be how you've been conditioned to do business. Traditional logic tells us, "I've got to be the strong leader who comes in to kick the salespeople's butts." What I've found to be much more effective, though, is to prioritize a highly functioning, highly effective team focused on mutual support and maintaining a sense of fun.

Part of why you picked up this book is because you want a healthy company culture, right?

Sure, you could probably hire somebody to come in and demand your sales team work long hours and spend all their time making cold calls. You could probably find a million books to read about how to do that. It would be easier than taking the unique strengths of each of your salespeople into account and building a thorough plan. Making these black-and-white demands on the team, though, is picking up a hammer and treating every problem like a nail. Eventually you're going to smash more holes into your organization (meaning, your best people will probably leave to find more gratifying work).

Ultimately, we're trying to build a better state, but both the architecture and the construction are going to evolve with input from the team. By the very nature of this work, you won't know exactly what that better state is on day one. You are going to discover it, but only if everyone else sees and cocreates the blueprints.

The Three Qualities of a Change Agent

As Change Agent, this person is not the expert, not the boss—they are a guide. The guide's job isn't to show up with the answer but to understand the problem. Business-minded people are usually critical thinkers who want to get into something and fix it, even before fully understanding the problem. On this journey, the Change Agent is going to be like an investigative reporter, asking questions until they're clear on what the conflicts are. The information they need to resolve those conflicts comes from the Improvement Team sharing their observations and the Change Agent being able to collect and put their thoughts into action.

Following are the three core qualities (in no particular order) a Change Agent needs to bring your sales organization into alignment. These are the guidelines to how this person should be present in this experience—and how you should be too. Keep in mind that whatever role you end up playing in the process of building your Revenue Equation, you'll need to help uphold each of these qualities. While the Change Agent is there to guide, everyone's cooperation is important to support the process.

Seek to Understand

Let's say you are living in some rural place, and there is no GPS on your phone. A stranger rolls up and says, "Hey, where's the nearest convenience store?" Until you can help them orient themselves to where they are in that moment, whatever directions you give them will probably be inaccurate. You need to have a common starting point. Without that, you can't get where you want to go.

Every quality of a Change Agent builds on this principle of having a common vantage point. This moderator and guide needs to prove to everyone that they truly value each person's opinion and that they're going to give them their full attention to make them feel understood at the deepest level possible. They need to prove to the team by walking the talk that they really value what the team has to say. The Change Agent—and you—might not agree with what's said, but it's not anyone's job to pass judgment.

One of the things that everyone wants most in life is to be understood. The Change Agent's job is to be a sponge and soak it up, then repeat it back until that person nods and says, "You get me."

SEEKING TO UNDERSTAND THE GROUP

Once I realized that United Events, the live events production company I referred to in the last chapter, was struggling with their company identity, I decided to run a workshop to help. Now, rather than just asking the CEO, I asked the six-person Improvement Team, "Why do people buy from you?"

One person said, "Because we partner with the customer."

Everyone agreed with one another, and soon all I heard from every participant was the word "partner." It was an idea I was used to hearing from clients, especially from companies in the events sector. But what did it *mean*?

As the Change Agent seeks to understand, it's vital that they continue to ask pointed questions. I knew that the word "partner" could mean something different to each of the six people in the room. Until we defined the word, we would not be starting from the same vantage point. We wouldn't be able to point to our location on a map and move toward creating a better state.

"Here's what 'partner' means to me," I said. "First, let me ask you this. Do you think marriage is a partnership?"

They all agreed that it was.

"So, when my wife and I got married and decided to have kids," I continued, "it was understood that I was going to focus on being the breadwinner and she was going to leave her job and focus on taking care of the kids. I remember that many times it was tough to stay in my lane. For instance, when my kids were really young and got sick, she'd be up all night. I'd be up late with her, helping take care of pukey kids, but then she'd tell me to go back to bed. She reminded me that her job was to take care of the kids and my job was to go to work in the morning to make sure we had enough money to keep the household going. Nights like that were hard, but she was right.

"To me, that's a partnership. We both brought something to it, and we both would make sacrifices for the other person when we needed to. Is that what you are doing with your customers?"

It's common for an organization to use language without examining what it really means, then move in different directions from one another without even knowing it. One person might have thought that to partner with a customer meant being available to them 24/7, while another might have perceived it to mean something much more surface level. If I hadn't stopped to dig deeper and get everyone to the same starting point, we may have continued to move forward using a word that meant very different things to each person. The Change Agent is there to listen to what's below the surface of the language an organization uses to find the real meaning and whether or not everyone understands and agrees on that meaning.

SEEKING TO UNDERSTAND THE INDIVIDUAL

While groupthink within an organization can provide multiple knots for a Change Agent to untie, there are also individuals within organizations who have distinct opinions about the way things should be done.

A Change Agent needs to be much more than just an active listener. They need to be able to deliver something that every person wants: true understanding. That doesn't just mean the Change Agent repeats things back to the person speaking. It means they pursue a line of questioning until the team member feels heard and understood. To do this, the Change Agent has to be extremely present in every conversation.

To keep the team on track, I like to ask, "What's showing up for you?" to get to the core of any given problem. The question is open-ended enough that it invites a wide range of thoughts and possibilities that help me understand what is happening. It could mean anything from "How does that statement make you feel?" to "Are you making any connections to what is being said right now?" to "Are any solutions coming to mind?" Every time I ask that question, it nudges me forward to a deeper understanding of the scenario I'm working within. I ask that question of the individual I'm talking to in addition to the group, and I ask it of myself to focus my understanding of what the team is saying to me.

Here's an example from when I had just started to work with the Improvement Team of Online Academy. I was in a meeting with the four salespeople, Maria, Lori, Alex, and Ted, and the marketing lead, Jasmine. We were starting to work through the Sales Foundations, and I asked Maria, "What problem do you think we solve?"

She said, "We solve the problem of giving someone a clear path forward to change their life."

Lori chimed in with "I thought we sold online training programs and business certifications."

Clearly, this was a misalignment that needed to be explored. I addressed the rest of the group. "So, Lori says that we sell online programs and business certifications, and Maria also pointed out that we solve a deeper problem. What's showing up for you when she says that?"

The question, "What is showing up for you?" is not just a way to help the Change Agent get to the bottom of an issue. Asking it aloud also helps people in the rest of the group understand their own roles and fill in missing pieces. It's also open-ended enough that it can draw input from the introverts in the room, and it can be useful when there is tension in the group or someone becomes frustrated.

Jasmine said, "Actually, what Maria is saying is exactly what we've been saying on our blog."

"We have a blog??" Ted asked.

I saw Jasmine's expression, and I asked her, "What's showing up for you?"

She said, "What's shown up for me is that we better get some better communication going between sales and marketing because we're selling two completely different things."

As a guide, the Change Agent is asking open-ended questions, looking for the Improvement Team to reflect back on their experiences with their observations, feelings, critiques, and ideas. The guide says, *We now have all had the same experience where we've heard everyone share; what is your individual experience?* As the guide, the more a Change Agent facilitates, the more they can recognize and hear each individual experience and repeat it back to them.

At this point in my conversation with the Online Academy team, I had absorbed that Jasmine had been experiencing frustration, but I also didn't place blame on anybody else for that frustration.

"So, Jasmine," I said, "what I think you just told me was you don't think marketing really gets sales. And your conclusion is that if we don't fix that, we're going to continue to have a problem."

"Exactly," Jasmine said.

Because we'd been able to get to the bottom of this misalignment with no fights and no judgments, the next person who shared knew it was okay to be honest about what was showing up for them. This neutral way of pursuing an idea to its roots is the way to fully utilize all the insight that your Improvement Team can provide.

Hold the Vision

The Change Agent has brought a group of individuals together to find their starting place. They have held up the map, drawn a big circle around the vantage point, and said, "You are here."

As the team starts developing every piece of the Revenue Equation, the Change Agent keeps their hands firmly on that map. The Change Agent does not venture into this experience without knowing, and keeping their eyes on, where the journey is meant to go. The territory everyone will cover together will always be full of surprises, so when the group hits a roadblock, or one or more individuals begin to wander off the trail, the Change Agent is the one who pulls out the compass and brings everyone back to define their new vantage point.

An Improvement Team may have gone through the ritual of creating a mission statement or a vision statement. They may have done a lot of exercises meant to define the business's identity. Relying on just those tactics, however, is like buying a map, giving it a quick glance, then leaving it at home and assuming you can get where you want to go without it.

Stepping out onto the trail and then staying on the path until you reach your destination is a process of recommitting to your journey over and over again. Sometimes a Change Agent is simply reminding everyone what's been covered so far, but they can also offer a response to a major or minor hiccup.

I started working with United Events in July and August. During those months, they had a lot of time to devote to the process of improving their sales organization. September through December, however, was a busy season for them with a ton of events, so we moved from larger meetings to a few one-on-ones just to keep up-to-date and moving toward our desired state.

By November, we had worked through the entire Revenue Equation. We had built up a good amount of trust, and everyone was already starting to see improvements, but people were so busy that they were starting to cancel meetings and not do the assigned work.

The leadership team, however, was still trying to put some major changes in place, and they decided to roll out a really big change that backfired hard. Overnight, the salespeople were asked to completely change the way they tracked their time. Because I wasn't around nearly as much as I had been in the summer, it was as big of a surprise to me as it was to them.

When I talked to the leadership team, they insisted that everyone had known the time tracking change was coming.

"If I have five people who are all telling me that they didn't know this was coming," I said, "you didn't tell them, you didn't tell them often enough, or you didn't get their commitment."

All that was true, and it required damage control, but I was also calling them out on something that I should have done myself. A Change Agent needs to ask both the leadership team and the sales teams to recommit to the process regularly. You need vocal confirmation from each person on what they're doing, why they're doing it, and whether it's something they're still committed to working on.

That was what we ended up doing at United Events, gathering everyone together for a group heart-to-heart. This meant the salespeople were able to voice their frustrations and the leadership team was able to acknowledge those frustrations and resolve to do better in the future.

Even if you know where you are at the beginning of your journey, that doesn't mean you won't get off track from time to time. On a trip, when you reach crossroads, you need to check your map to make sure you're making the correct turn. The Change Agent needs to have these checkpoints where they help people remember why they are doing this work, ask whether they can continue to commit to following through with it, and suggest how, if they've gone in the wrong direction, they can get back on track.

Consistently Build Trust

When a company is struggling with misalignments, people may experience negative feelings and thoughts they're reluctant to share. When the Improvement Team feels inhibited, it's harder to draw out the insights that could improve the organization the most. That's why the Change Agent needs to foster an environment in which everyone can comfortably express themselves without fear. This is done by maintaining confidentiality and creating spaces that are safe for each person to be open and honest.

First, team members should be confident that what they say will be respected and kept in confidence. Let's say I have a one-on-one with a salesperson, and they pour their heart out about their frustrations. Then a few days later one of their superiors approaches them and says, "I heard that you were unhappy about something." I would have violated that person's confidence, like I was tattling on them to the teacher. After that, the salesperson would be reluctant to tell me anything other than what they think their boss would want them to say. Once you lose trust, you might as well lose the expectation that they'll contribute anything that could lead to lasting change.

Beyond that, the way to cultivate a safe environment is something that the Change Agent has to determine on their own. Would small groups work the best? One-on-one meetings? Maybe people can work in a group, then have breakout sessions where the Change Agent has one-on-ones with the more reserved members of the team. The way to determine this is by listening, observing, and asking what the best conditions would be for each of these individuals to feel heard and understood.

When I got to Online Academy, I discovered that Maria and Lori had been butting heads for months. Creating an environment where both of them felt that they could express themselves safely took some creative thinking.

One month, Lori was having some struggles in her personal life, and because of that, her sales had suffered. In one meeting, I wanted her to be able to share without making her feel guilty or putting her on the spot. I decided to design a meeting that would facilitate that for her, without her knowing. Since she was having a hard time already, if I had said, "Lori, let's have a meeting where everyone can give you tips to get your sales up," that may have offended her or made her feel guiltier. That's exactly what I wanted to avoid.

In the meeting, each of the four salespeople was allotted five minutes to speak about the way that each of them ran their sales calls. I laid down ground rules so the salespeople knew that when they spoke, they would not be interrupted. The truncated amount of speaking time may have seemed counterintuitive. I gave them less time to talk so they had to focus on expressing what was important to them, rather than addressing what someone else had previously said. I intentionally did not make it an open dialogue.

Choosing who would speak first was also important. I intentionally had Lori go last. Maria had been killing it with her sales for the past three months, and based on their history, I knew that hearing about Maria's success right up top might make it hard for Lori to be fully present. Instead, I chose Alex, who had a friendly, positive attitude and a straightforward approach and who was so organized that he had a record of every sales call he had ever made. He kept a folder of marketing materials, blog articles, and PDFs that he could use to meet the customer at whatever point in their buyer's journey they happened to be.

Alex excitedly described how he walked prospects through the sales presentation, asked them if they needed anything else to make a decision, and then followed up with what they asked for as soon as possible (logging each step in his CRM immediately afterward, of course).

I repeated what he said, to make sure I had understood, then thanked him and moved on.

Maria spoke next. Despite Lori's friction with her, I wanted her to learn from Maria and be able to draw some value from what she was saying. I intentionally had Maria speak second, leaving one salesperson in between the two of them as a buffer.

"I don't know what I'm doing," Maria said, "but whatever it is, it's working great." I knew that Maria had a side hustle as a part-time life coach, and when I questioned further, I determined that she was approaching her prospects with a similar coach-y touch. She shared that she spoke in story arcs during sales calls, incorporating the program the organization was selling as a vital turning point in the story of that prospect's life.

After I summarized what Maria said, next up was Ted, who had a more freeform approach than Alex and Maria. Additionally, he and Lori had worked together for a while and were on really good terms with one another. He'd be an easier act for her to follow.

"I like to build rapport," Ted said. "I joke around a little first and then get into the sales presentation." He went on to share his process for the rest of his allotted time. I repeated what I'd heard from him, he agreed, and I moved on to Lori.

As I'd predicted, Lori was comfortable enough to talk freely by the time we reached her. She'd seen how focused the conversation was (constructive, nonjudgmental, and safe for all) and how free the others had been to speak without interruption. "I gotta admit—I've been off my game the last three or four weeks," she said. "Everything you guys have said here is helping me a ton."

Instead of reprimanding her for her lower sales, I gave her some encouragement for being so honest. It worked. Lori opened up about some new ideas she was having, and they were great ideas that helped everyone in the meeting. Before we wrapped up, each of the salespeople was in a good spirit, saying, "This was a great call. We should do this again."

In the end, I'd been successful in what I set out to do. The way I designed the meeting had created the space for everyone to feel safe sharing, brainstorming, and helping one another. Lori had provided the whole team with value because of how she'd shown up and diagnosed her own problem. This experience demonstrates several ways that the Change Agent can create a safe environment where everyone will be able to bring their best to the table.

1. **Understand the team as individuals.** Because I'd taken time to get to know each of the four salespeople, I predicted in general how each of them would describe how they run a call. It also meant that I could create circumstances that would serve the salesperson who was in the greatest need of help in that moment. Throughout the meeting, I verbally confirmed with each person that I'd understood them by repeating back what they had said.

2. **Clearly set intentions.** At the beginning of the call, I left nothing to the imagination. Every person knew how long the meeting would be, how long they would have to speak, and that they would neither be interrogated nor be permitted to interrogate anyone else. Within those constraints, the team was able to feel the freedom of using their uninterrupted time to talk about their processes and really be themselves.

3. **Establish a judgment-free zone.** Lori opened up about how she was having a hard time caring about her work and that her sales had been suffering because of it, which is a tough thing to admit to people. If I had then lectured her in front of the rest of the team (or even in a one-on-one), there's a chance she never would have been that honest with me again, and I would have lost her vital, uncensored input.

I have the best results when I get the Improvement Team to focus on an objective that they all think will help them individually and as a group, addressing something they all agree is a problem. This way, there's no blame being placed on anyone. It's the company, not them, that needs to be fixed.

As we progress through the different elements of the Revenue Equation, and eventually their Individual Performance Planners, they then start to realize, "You know what—I didn't know this," and they start to connect these discussions to ways they can improve their own sales. They feel comfortable enough to think about what they could be doing better because they feel supported and involved enough that their own actions might actually make a difference in the company's growth.

That kind of realization is a lot more effective than the Change Agent shaming them and saying, "I can't believe you didn't know these things! They're on page twelve of the company handbook!"

What the Improvement Team, both individually and collectively, starts to see is that the Change Agent is truly trying to improve the sales organization. They also see that a byproduct of the process is that it is going to improve their individual lives. Once everyone has agreed on the direction to take the conversation as a sales organization, the Change Agent can switch the focus to the individual level and say, "Okay, now that we've done that, let's see if we can help you be the best you can be." If the Change Agent can continue to hold that space, they will be able to grow the cohesiveness, the positivity, and the performance of everyone involved.

Am I the Change Agent?

Check the box to the left of every statement that applies to you.

- ☐ I have ten hours available per week to meet with people and process information.
- ☐ I have the authority to organize meetings and require prework from team members.

- ☐ I can commit to always seeking to understand individuals on the team.
- ☐ The team will trust me to keep their information confidential.
- ☐ The team will trust me enough to respond honestly to my questions.
- ☐ The team is comfortable pointing things out to me without damaging my ego.
- ☐ I know or can learn active listening and investigative techniques.
- ☐ I have the discipline to ask the team to regularly recommit to the process of organizational change.

If you can say yes to all of those, Change Agent is probably a role you can take on yourself (though it might be good to check in with another person on your leadership team in case they can see any barriers you may have overlooked). Even if not, keep reading—your position, whatever it may end up being, will be greatly improved by understanding how you can best support the Change Agent as they guide your organization through this period of transformation.

Chapter 3:
Are You Ready for Change?

Preparing the Players for Action

Let's say that you're a Decision Maker, someone who is in a position of leadership, and your company has finally given up on treating symptoms and ignoring their root causes. You're not looking for that magic spell that will break the curse on your company. You now know that there is a deeply ingrained problem in your sales organization that needs to be addressed and that it's possible for you to transform into a sales organization that is positive, effective, and committed to the well-being and performance of both the team and the individual. You also know that a Change Agent is the best person to lead you through making this happen for yourself and your people.

The problem is maybe you're not sure that you're the person who can do that work. You might already be working seven days a week and barely taking time for yourself. How could you possibly squeeze leading in-depth meetings and aggregating and synthesizing information into that equation?

Or maybe the obstacle that you are facing is that you're more of a hands-off type of leader. You're good at delegating work, and you do your own work well, but the idea of rolling up your sleeves and getting your hands dirty isn't really appealing to you.

Neither means you need to give up on strengthening your sales organization. If you are in a position of leadership in your company where you can achieve long-lasting positive change, you still have an important role to play.

In order for the Change Agent to be able to do this work, they are going to need an ally who has the power to give them what they need to do it. I call this person the Champion. While the Change Agent plays a pivotal role in guiding the work of transforming an organization, their effectiveness will be limited without the Champion.

The Champion is the person who sees the problem and has the power to delegate solving it. It is vital that the Champion be able to provide two key resources to the Change Agent so they can do their job.

Resource 1: Ample Time to Work

Providing time for the Change Agent to work through each step of the process is a must. They'll need an allotment of hours to focus on the process every week. Those hours need to be consistently doled out through the entirety of your transformation process. For me, that is three to six months, at the very least, but usually more like nine to twelve, with an average commitment of ten hours per week.

If you are assigning a Change Agent, they need to be someone who is not already working at full capacity or, if they are, can hand over some of their responsibilities to someone else. Leading a sales organization through change requires time to meet with members of the Improvement Team one-on-one as well as in a group setting. The Change Agent also needs time alone to process all the information that's coming from these meetings and to create the tools that your team will be using to build your sales organization's new standard operating procedures.

Resource 2: A Reasonable Level of Authority

The most important thing that the Change Agent needs from a Champion is right there in their title: agency. You can also think of it as giving them authority, specifically, to call meetings, pull people away from other work they're doing, and maintain confidential communication with employees. They will also be assigning employees work to do individually, so they'll need to have the confidence that the Champion is providing employees with time to focus on that.

As the Champion, you also must be able to back up the Change Agent when they require prework or presence from employees and allow them to hold you accountable for work they need from you. If required, you should also be ready to appoint someone to support the Change Agent in taking notes and processing information.

Assigning a Change Agent

If you are a Champion who is looking for someone within your own organization to act as Change Agent, they'll need to possess the three qualities we discussed in chapter 2.

You need to ensure that the person you choose can hold the vision and intention for months full of inquiry and introspection. This person needs to be willing to seek to understand everyone involved in building the Three Frameworks. You need to trust and respect this person enough to allow them to speak with other employees confidentially, to give them (and you!) work to complete, and to use the allotted time productively.

If you feel that those in sales or marketing leadership are too close to the problem, you can do what some Decision Makers have done and bring in someone from a different department to lead the conversations. Maybe your VP of finance or operations manager has the skills and distance from the problem to do this work. If they can't do it all themselves, you can assign another member of your staff to give administrative support like note taking and information processing. If you know there are people in your organization who fit this description, and you are happy to give them the time and authority they'll need, go have a chat with them (and make sure to give them a copy of this book).

Maybe you're in a place where nobody can spare the time to do the work, or maybe relationships within the team itself are too volatile to choose someone to lead the charge. Hiring someone from outside the company is also the job of the Champion. You'll need to be ready to grant the same authority and time with the team that would be given to an internal Change Agent and put whatever safeguards in place so that you can trust them with private information. Either way, throughout this process, the Change Agent and the Champion will be in close communication with each other to make sure people don't wander away from this transformational path.

Always Debrief the Mayor

Now that we've laid out what the Champion needs to provide to the Change Agent, let's flip those roles around. Let's talk about what the Change Agent needs to do to maintain a good relationship with the Champion and other Decision Makers in the organization.

I live in a small town and used to be on the board of the urban renewal authority. Traditionally, the mayor ran that board, but when Mayor Chuck left, the new mayor decided he wanted one of the other commissioners to run the meetings versus being the chair himself. I was appointed.

Like any other community, we've had our fair share of controversial issues to deal with. One involved us coming up with an alternative way for the renewal authority to partner with the City on a development project. With taxes, developers, contractors, and government players involved, it had the potential to become a political situation. I'd come up with a way of funding it that hadn't really been tried before, and if you know anything about small towns, you know you have to be really careful about how you frame a new way of doing things.

For the meeting where we were presenting my idea, I'd asked a couple staff members from the City to present to the board. We already basically knew what we wanted to do, but we needed to socialize the idea, make sure everyone understood it, and then look for buy-in. While I was pretty confident it was a good plan and would have some support, there was still an element of the unknown.

A couple of days before I did this, however, I got a call from Chuck. He gave me a piece of advice that has served me very well when working to bring about change not just in my community but in every sales organization I've worked with.

"Karl," he said, "whenever you have a new idea on the table that doesn't have buy-in yet, you need to tell the mayor what you're going to cover that day. Make sure you provide visibility of what you want to do and what possible points of contention may come up. Don't put him in a place where he feels unprepared."

That had never occurred to me before. Of course the mayor would want to be in the know; he was the one who would have the most exposure to the media and the rest of the community if something went wrong or was badly received.

When I hung up with the former mayor, my next call was to the current mayor. I let him know what we would be discussing, what my plan was for presenting it, and how I thought other people on the board might react. He was grateful to me for giving him a heads up about what was going to be happening, and I was grateful to Chuck for pointing out something that, in the worst case, could break someone's trust and damage an important relationship.

Part of the Change Agent's "seeking to understand" that we discussed in chapter 2 is observing group dynamics and anticipating what effects these changes might have on people. The Change Agent needs to know who has the most exposure at a company. Who is going to catch the most flack if there's some kind of conflict, and who is going to be stuck picking up the pieces if something breaks? Using this knowledge with care is an important part of maintaining trust with Decision Makers and the Improvement Team, and it helps ensure success and positive change.

Say the Change Agent has a session with just the Improvement Team with no Decision Makers participating. In this scenario, the team has felt comfortable enough to air some of their grievances. Maybe it's so many grievances that the Change Agent knows it's going to be tough for the Decision Makers at the company to hear when they inevitably are called back in. As the Change Agent seeks to understand and create an environment of trust and safety, they need to prepare the Decision Makers for what is about to happen without betraying the rest of the Improvement Team's confidence

For example, I didn't tell Dave, the CEO of Online Academy, "Hey, guess what? Turns out Maria really doesn't agree with the direction you're taking this company." That would have been betraying Maria's trust, and it wouldn't have been useful. Instead, I let him know that the tone of the meeting would be challenging, and he might hear some things that he might not like.

The Change Agent can let the company's Decision Makers know some of the critiques that they heard without throwing anyone under the bus, and they should prime the Decision Makers on how to respond to that type of feedback without becoming defensive.

To consistently build trust, the Change Agent has to prepare every person to have uncomfortable conversations that, when done successfully, will result in valuable insights and bring the team closer together. Preparing the Decision Makers is a unique responsibility, especially if they are founders (this company is their baby, after all).

Additionally, if there is more than one Decision Maker, the Change Agent needs to ensure that each one is in alignment with the other before proceeding to work with the team. If Decision Makers don't align, the whole process could get torpedoed before it even leaves port.

Trust me. I've been caught in the crossfire before.

When Leaders Don't Align

Let's say I wanted to take a road trip to Los Angeles from Denver with my family. I might want to go check out Las Vegas on the way. But maybe my wife would rather go south and visit San Diego first. Either way, the two trips both have the same destination.

But if I want to go to LA and the rest of my family wants to go to Seattle, there's no room for compromise. We have to choose one person's preference over the other, part ways and take two different road trips, or stay home.

When you have leaders who have their eyes on completely different objectives, ones that are so different that they're not even on the same latitude, it's going to be difficult to accomplish any of them. That's why, if you are a Change Agent working with more than one Decision Maker, there has to be consensus before you bring in the rest of the team.

THERE ARE SOMETIMES MAJOR OBSTACLES to stabilizing and growing revenue. One of the most irreparable, though, is when leaders are not aligned.

I had flown out to work with a SaaS company (a software as a service company) on their Revenue Equation, facilitating development of their values, differentiators, offerings, and target audience and making sure the team was aligned and could move forward more effectively.

There were two Decision Makers at this company: Phil and Derrick. Phil was the company founder and president, a former New York shopkeeper who found a way to help small-businesses owners automate transactions to help them save money. Derrick had been a frequent patron of Phil's shop and had offered to be an early investor for the new company, as long as he was appointed CEO. Since Derrick had more experience in the business world, Phil was happy to have the help and guidance. Phil moved their headquarters out of the city to save money and ran day-to-day operations. Derrick continued to live and work in New York and flew in once a month to meet with him.

Unfortunately, when it came to the way the business worked, the two did not align. Their sales were stagnating, and they needed to scale up in order to survive. The company's sales manager had heard me speak at a conference and had contacted me in hopes that I could help focus the company and steer it onto a better path to sales growth, and the two Decision Makers had at least agreed to give the idea a try.

In our first meeting, Derrick exuded judgment, leaning against the wall with his arms crossed and furrowing his brow. I started with the Revenue Equation Diagnostic, a quiz that I use to gauge everyone's understanding of the company's Sales Foundations, Sales Design, and Sales Infrastructure (all of which we'll talk more about starting in the next chapter). As the meeting went on and gaps in the Improvement Team's understanding of the business started to show, Derrick seemed to take the idea that changes were needed very personally.

As he became more agitated, Phil reminded him, "Derrick, we talked about this already, and I thought we'd agreed this was the right decision to improve sales."

But there were more arguments beyond whether they needed to do these exercises or not. They couldn't agree on whether they should work with the offerings they had or create new ones. They couldn't decide what language to use when describing the value they offered customers. It was as if all their business's inner demons, as well as their own personal insecurities, were spilling out in front of everyone in the room.

Over the next several weeks, we continued to work, and as the Change Agent, I assigned work to different teams and team members. Derrick rarely did his part and didn't attend the majority of the meetings, often out of town at his other job, and consistently communicated that Phil should call the shots. The rest of us did our best to work through the different factors of the Revenue Equation and start developing sales strategies that could help the company scale.

However, when Derrick would come back to town to attend our meetings, he was often unhappy with the results he saw. Phil, the

Improvement Team, and I had written out and agreed upon the company's Sales Foundations, Sales Design, and Sales Infrastructure, but when Derrick saw our work, he took issue with the language we used and the strategies we'd developed. It was frustrating that we had agreed on everything and Derrick had supposedly authorized Phil to call the shots, but then he wouldn't agree with our solutions. I began to doubt that the Improvement Team was able to truly give honest input with all the conflicting messages they were getting.

There was so much discord, so much disagreement between Phil and Derrick, that the whole engagement was compromised. I divined from our conversations with the two of them that when things were working out, they would get along. If they weren't making money, though, then they would start to point fingers rather than getting to the root of the problem.

I have no doubt that each Decision Maker at this company cared passionately about their success. As CEO and an early investor, Derrick had an enormous personal stake in the business. It was natural he'd be a little anxious. However, if your Decision Makers aren't walking in step, you're never going to have a high-performing sales organization. If you do, it's going to be by luck, not by intentionality, and you can't count on it to be sustainable.

Are Your Decision Makers on the Same Page?

Before going any further, you need to determine whether your Decision Makers are going to be able to work together—both with each other and with the Improvement Team—to create a better state. I suggest that your leaders sit down to answer the following questions, then compare answers after the fact.

- What is our company's purpose?
- What are our values?
- What do we want the company to look like in three years?

Five years?
- What do we think is working well right now?
- Where do we think we need improvements?

If you don't know the answers to these questions, that's okay. If the Decision Makers have different answers, that's okay too. These questions are the most important part of this lesson because your answers create a common starting point.

If you are unsure how to move forward, ask the Change Agent to moderate a discussion about your answers. Make sure you are aligned and get in agreement before involving the rest of the team.

Ground Rules for Leadership

The best course of action with Phil and Derrick's SaaS company was to name the problem and be honest about the consequences. If the Decision Makers are not solid about where they're going with the business, any money that they put forward is at risk (plus, their conflict could have a pretty toxic effect on the company's culture). Carrying out marketing campaigns, selling more, and earning higher revenues don't make the business sustainable, and that means that bringing in revenue could be as effective as continuing to fill a leaky bucket with more water.

Misaligned leadership is sadly common. At the SaaS company, several people had invested millions of dollars and felt that they could call the shots. This misaligned leadership can also take other forms, such as in the family business, where maybe the founder's child has taken over operations, and their parent is "semiretired" but still owns a major share. Power dynamics there are tricky, and while the founder may not be in charge in title, nobody wants to upset them or question their authority.

When it comes to the components of the Revenue Equation, there needs to be someone who gives the final word, even when more than one person is in leadership. Part of giving the Change Agent authority is allowing them to make some of the decisions, but it needs to be understood from the beginning who gives the final go-ahead. Otherwise the Change Agent will be trying to feed a multiheaded monster, with all of the heads fighting over the same plate.

If the Change Agent does end up in this sort of situation, however, it's not enough to carry on without acknowledging the problem. No matter how well they facilitate a meeting, if no decisions are made, if there's no consensus on the final product, the work is not complete. It's the job of the Change Agent to maintain that boundary. It's all part of their responsibility to hold the vision—at every fork in the road, someone needs to say decisively which way to turn, because otherwise there's no reaching the summit.

The fact is, the Decision Makers are going to have disagreements, even if they are mostly aligned with one another and have mechanisms in place to solve conflicts. I have yet to see a situation where Decision Makers are in complete lockstep from beginning to end. All of this work is predicated on the fact that the company is not in alignment. Every participant who comes to the table has a different idea of what the company is supposed to be.

The Change Agent, as they create an environment of safety and trust, can set clear standards for leadership to hold together and for the participants to have confidence that their work will bear fruit. It just takes a little bit of prework.

Balancing Flexibility and Decisiveness

Even if they're not being obstructionist, sometimes leaders can unintentionally make it difficult for a team to take action.

Josh, the CEO of Bay Area Games, had an entrepreneurial attitude, bending and adapting to a shifting environment, changing his mind constantly and agreeing to new opportunities to the point that he was overloading himself. While his ability to process and adapt quickly was an advantage, it also was creating challenges in aligning the team on a clearly defined path forward. Because of the lack of intentionality when bringing in brand partners, and without the commitment to fully testing their ideas, the company was at risk of running out of time to meet their goals for the next round of funding. The team had to be able to be in complete alignment with the action plan if they were to make their deadline, and they couldn't do that if their CEO couldn't focus.

There were three leaders of the company, and at first Josh wanted all three of them to be the Decision Makers. He was the main Decision Maker; the second was Rahul, cofounder with Josh as well as an engineer and VP of product, who had a laid-back, go-with-the-flow personality; the third was the VP of operations, Danny. He was the one with his foot on the brake, worrying about the budget and a lack of resources and responding to exercises with more anxiety than the others. His behavior was usually in direct contradiction to the CEO's attitude of saying yes to every new idea that crossed his path. While the CEO was the one with the authority to choose the direction, he wasn't really committing to a single course of action.

The Bay Area Games team came prepared to our first meeting, having completed the worksheets that I had provided for them in advance. Each member of the Improvement Team, including the Decision Makers, had not only done the prework but showed up to our workshops ready to collaborate and work together. This existing level of teamwork and openness to learning provided a head start to the effectiveness of our time working together, which was really important with how quickly we needed to bring in sales.

At one point, Josh asked me privately, "Hey, can you give me some feedback? How do you think I'm doing?"

I said, "Well, you're really inclusive and you listen to people and you really hear them, and your fault is the same as your strength. You keep saying yes, even though there's no plan, and so your focus area is getting wider and wider and wider, which makes the rest of the team unclear on where you are really going in this model."

After our talk, Josh put in a greater effort to use his role as Decision Maker to commit the group to clear courses of action. It made building the Revenue Equation and aligning the company much smoother, whether or not there were dissenting voices. Even the VP of operations was set way more at ease, finally able to see what path they were on. If I, the Change Agent, hadn't made it clear that Josh, as CEO, needed to own his role as the key Decision Maker, there could have been much more conflict when trying to divine the company's Sales Foundations, Sales Design, and Sales Infrastructure.

Change Agents shouldn't shy away from offering honest feedback to leadership. A lot of teams need their leaders to be clear in their decision-making so that they know which way to go, and the Decision Makers, especially ones who value working collaboratively, often need to be reminded of that.

Send in the Improvement Team... and Get Ready for Surprises

I recently went to the climbing gym with my twelve-year-old son Morgan. As soon as we arrived, he roped up with his climbing gear and went at it with full force.

For a solid hour, he scaled the walls, and I belayed. While we took turns climbing, he was on the walls the majority of the time. I was pretty impressed with him, since climbing takes a lot of focus, balance, and endurance. I didn't know where he got all his energy, but I also knew that eventually he'd run out of steam. When he popped off a tricky part of the route on the last climb and asked me to lower him down, I thought he'd reached that point.

That was when the joy of youth dropped in. While I thought it was going to be time to pack it in, he told me he was going to go over to the bouldering area. While I admired his passion, as his dad, I was a little worried about him. *My* arms and legs were toast, and he was the one who had done most of the climbing the last hour.

Up until this point, I had been climbing with him, and he'd been aided by ropes, but in the bouldering area, Morgan would now be free-climbing. The fake boulders were up about fifteen to twenty feet, with padding below. I opted not to argue with him, though. I didn't want to be the dad who jumped in to make a decision on behalf of his son. If he were to take a fall, he'd land on soft mats—though I cringed when I imagined him dropping from one of those fifteen-foot overhangs.

Sure enough, he went to one of the overhang routes. He gracefully made his way up with balance and control until the last five feet, where the overhang was really pronounced. His feet slipped off the wall, but he continued to hang on by arm strength alone. He swung there for a second or two as he maneuvered his feet back onto the small toeholds. A few seconds later, he had moved gracefully through the overhang and to the top of the climb. He turned around with a huge grin on his face that matched the smile on mine. A proud parent moment and a lesson all in one.

I was dumbfounded—this kid I thought had already worn himself out had stepped up to the one of the toughest boulders at the gym and literally come out on top.

If he had come down from the climbing wall and been clearer with me about his exact intentions—"Hey, Dad, I want to go climb *that* boulder"—how would I have reacted? Would I have hovered at the base of the boulder to make sure he didn't fall? Would I have discouraged him and said, "Nah, you're tired. Let's just go home?" I honestly don't know, but it's possible that I could have intervened and prevented him from having that experience. And it would have deprived me of the joy of having a major proud-dad moment.

The experience of being pleasantly surprised happens again and again when I run, cultivate, and coach teams as a Change Agent. I have no idea what surprises any one of the members of the Improvement Team might bring. I've had the lowest-performing salesperson come up with a solution that kicked a stagnant conversation back into gear.

If I had excluded low-performing salespeople from the meeting, I never would have gotten the jewel of their insight.

Whatever part you're playing, you may have some existing feelings about your salespeople. Maybe you think the reason your company is having trouble with revenue is because they're lazy or simply not that great at their jobs. Starting this work with a group of people you already know can make it difficult for you to have that humble beginner's mindset and come to the work with openness and without prejudice.

Whether you are the Change Agent, the Champion, or one of the Decision Makers, I want to encourage you to keep your plans flexible and your preconceptions at a minimum. Let your team surprise you. Let all the participants surprise you. If everyone is going to go toward the same destination, toward stabilized and increased revenue, then you need to really hold the space to allow that to happen. They each have a different experience of their jobs and the company itself that you probably hadn't even considered before.

I ran a team training with two of the salespeople from Online Academy, Alex and Maria. This was still when I was new to working with them, and you might recall that I had been told the sales team's performance was the main thing that needed improvement. I was priming myself to see how steep their learning curve would be. The point of this meeting was for them to share strategies and tactics with one another regarding how they organize their time and keep track of their prospects. I was unsure of how much I was going to have to teach them, but I decided to start by giving them more space to respond to one another and see what they could do on their own.

As it turned out, they both had some really strong habits to stay organized. While they both came at managing their prospect lists from different directions, they were each able to appreciate the value of the other person's system. (Maria, for instance, was vocal in admiring Alex's meticulous use of the CRM to keep track of his ongoing follow-ups and lead-nurturing). While I did interject some prompting questions, I didn't have to push either of them to understand, empathize with the other, or learn from one another. They did that on their own. I didn't have much to add at all.

A big part of the process of building your high-performing sales organization is about centering the Improvement Team and appreciating and leveraging their individual personalities. This isn't about deciding who is "good" and who is "bad" on your team. Going through these Three Frameworks of improving your sales organization is about unlocking the power of your team and the individuals within the team.

If your organization is struggling, your people might feel stressed out, and nobody is at their best when they're stressed. However, once they are given the room to grow, to see what their roles are, and to learn how they can perform to their fullest, they relax and demonstrate amazing qualities nobody could have predicted. And that's what you want—a functioning team in a healthy company culture, working to create value and make your entire company better.

If you'd asked me if my twelve-year-old could eat the hardest boulder at the gym like candy, I probably would have said no. If you'd asked me at the beginning of working with Online Academy if the salespeople would end up being so generous with one another and genuinely interested in improving their systems, I would have been slow to say yes. But the truth is, we don't know what others are capable of, and that goes for our teams too. So, let's create this space, be open to the new ideas, and let ourselves be surprised and inspired.

Framework #1:
The Revenue Equation

Chapter 4:
The Revenue Equation

Assessing the Factors That Make Your Business Successful

Over the years, I have worked with many different companies in many different industries. One thing that naturally occurs is referrals to other companies within the same industry as your clients. One such referral I received early in the development of my Revenue Equation framework was with another live events company called Midwest Event Production. The first week that I worked with this event production company, their Champion asked me to sit down with the Improvement Team. I introduced myself and started in on the introductory session.

This was before I had really developed my version of the Revenue Equation Diagnostic as it currently stands, so instead of using the worksheets that I do now, I started off with a simple question:

"What is an existing brand out there that you think is like yours?"

The idea was to go around the table and ask each person what they thought, get a couple of ideas, and explore them further to start figuring out who this company really was.

The first person I asked replied, "Costco." When I asked her why, she said, "Well, we have everything the customer needs, and we have great prices, just like Costco."

Being new to working with this company, I had no reason to doubt that what she said was true. I thanked her and moved on to the next person at the table.

When I asked him what company he thought they were like, he replied, "The Ritz-Carlton."

I paused. I couldn't think of a company more different from Costco than the Ritz-Carlton. I asked him to continue.

"The Ritz-Carlton is about creating an amazing, unique experience for their guests, and they empower their employees to do whatever it takes to make a guest happy. I feel like we're like that. When somebody has an event that we work on, I really want to learn what experience they want to have and then work really hard to create that experience."

As Change Agent, I'm there seeking to understand. At this moment, though, I could tell it was going to take a lot more discussion to determine what this company was really about. I turned to the next person at the table.

After hearing those two completely conflicting statements, the next salesperson sat thinking carefully about how to answer. We all waited for an uncomfortably long time in silence.

Finally, he said, "We're like United Airlines."

United Airlines had been getting some bad press at the time, so I was kind of surprised to hear that. "Why are you like United Airlines?" I asked.

"Or Southwest, or any airline, really. I just mean, when you have an event, we take you where you need to go, just like an airline does." He was talking about airlines in general rather than a specific brand. I thanked him and moved on to the fourth team member, hoping another opinion would provide clarity.

"We're like the little wine shop I go to around the corner from my house," he said. "There are these wine experts who work there, and when I have a friend over for a nice dinner, I'll go over to the shop, and they help me choose the right wine to buy. I feel like I'm a wine expert but for the event industry. I learn the type of event you want to have, and then I make a recommendation on how to achieve the outcomes you want."

It was fascinating how misaligned this team was. They were totally unclear on the value that their company offered. The first person thought they sold on price, like Costco. The second was focused on creating exceptional experiences, like the Ritz-Carlton. The guy who was talking about airlines didn't seem clear on what made the company special at all. The last guy was more aligned with the one who compared the company to the Ritz-Carlton, in that he focused on a customized, tailored outcome for the customer, but the scope was much smaller.

Two of these salespeople moved on from the company not long after we worked through their version of the Revenue Equation. Can you guess which ones?

When the salesperson who compared the company to Costco left, she also left behind her customers to be inherited by the other salespeople. Those customers soon moved on as well because she had been selling based on price rather than providing a unique customer experience the way that the next salesperson did.

This underscores the importance of having everyone on the same page about who you are as a company, what you are selling, who you are selling to, and how you are selling it. If each of your team members is operating under completely different understandings of those elements (or if they don't really have an understanding at all), you are going to continue to miss out on the kind of business you really want to be doing, and the kinds of customers that you really want to have.

Measuring Perceptions on Your Team with the Revenue Equation

Sales Foundations + Sales Design + Sales Infrastructure = Revenue Stabilization and Growth

The kickoff activity when you're building your highly profitable sales organization is getting clear on the concept of the Revenue Equation. The Revenue Equation is a construction based on understanding the root causes of an organization's problems and the systems that will solve them. To reach the final goal of bringing in the revenue that you want, you'll need the whole organization to get to an 80 percent or higher level of mastery of the Sales Foundations, Sales Design, and Sales Infrastructure of your business.

Before we get ahead of ourselves by diving into how to solve your equation, the first step is to diagnose the problem. It's the Change Agent's job to trace the path forward, hold the vision of the destination, and then keep everyone together as you go. No one can go about tackling that main problem without a plan; you can't just start walking and be sure that you're going to get where you want to go.

What I'm about to describe to you is slightly more systematized than going around the table to ask each person what brand they think compares to their own. A more standardized exercise called the Revenue Equation Diagnostic helps identify where misfires are happening. It asks participants to evaluate their organization in the following areas:

Sales Foundations: These are the problems your company solves, the value you create, what differentiates you from other companies, your offerings, and what kind of experience you provide your customers.

Sales Design: Here, you design your approach to sales by determining the type of customers you sell your solutions to, what is important to them, and why these customers buy your solutions.

Sales Infrastructure: This is how you organize, operate, manage, and optimize your sales organization.

First, I have everyone on the Improvement Team fill out the Revenue Equation Diagnostic, including the Decision Makers. They in particular might be surprised at the ratings that team members give, and this exercise can be one of the first that opens people's eyes to the specific roots of their misalignments. The core purpose of the diagnostic is to seek to understand everyone's level of alignment, make sure the whole group understands how these foundations intersect, and go from there to redefine the company's Revenue Equation.

And bonus! Developing common understanding from doing this one exercise is going to have a major positive impact on your company. It provides an opportunity for teaming and the first chance for the Decision Makers to benefit from the Improvement Team's feedback and insights for how the company can become more aligned.

Moderating the Process as the Change Agent

Just as you, if you are the Change Agent, will be helping this company work according to their Sales Foundations, you'll also need to set ground rules for yourself. That's why every time you lead an exercise, you need to remember to be guided by the three qualities of the Change Agent. Here are some ways that might present

Holding the Vision

At the beginning of every exercise, it's vital that you be intentional and share what will be happening with all the participants right up top. You'll need to form answers to the following questions:

- Where are we going?
- How are we going to get there?
- What is expected of each participant?

Starting off with these answers will orient you as the person leading the conversation and ground everyone else.

Imagine you are planning a family vacation. To create the best possible outcome, I would start by answering those same three questions before taking off for adventure.

First off, where are we going? Let's say that the final destination is Washington, DC. Just knowing the destination isn't enough, though. I'll also need to consider a number of what you might call sub-destinations, such as the Smithsonian Institution, the National Mall, the Lincoln Memorial, and the White House.

Next, we decide how we'll get there, and we need to answer that question for each of the participants. We form a lot of our trips around the work I do, so I would probably fly out first on my own, and my wife would fly out with the kids afterward. We'll also need to answer the question for each of the sub-destinations. That means figuring out whether to rent a car, take Lyfts or Ubers around town, or rent bicycles. We'll need to figure out what time we're visiting each of the monuments we've agreed on and make room for the downtime that we'll undoubtedly need.

Last, we need to know our roles and responsibilities for each of the tasks. Who buys the plane tickets? Who researches the venues to figure out the best time to go and how much money to expect to spend? What are the backup plans that we need to follow when unexpected situations crop up? Of course, for the sake of everyone's comfort and happiness, everyone needs to be able to give their input throughout the trip about what to do, where to go, and when we need to take breaks.

When you do this for your team, you need to set out the big-picture goal, the ultimate destination, first, and then lay out all of the smaller sub-destinations that you'll be reaching along the way. You can use the information in chapter 1 as your guide to give an overview of the Three Frameworks they can look forward to completing.

Next, do the same thing on a micro level and talk about the goal of whatever subject you'll be tackling, how long it should take to get through, and all the topics you want to discuss. Ideally, for the Revenue Equation Diagnostic, you'll have had them do the assessment in advance (you can access it for no additional cost at revenueequation.com) and asked them to come ready to share their results. If you do have them do this prework, they'll know exactly what to expect from the meeting and what topics they're being asked to address.

Once you finish laying out how the process is going to go, in the short and long terms, give everyone time to bring up their questions and concerns. Remember that you, the Change Agent, are responsible for making sure they know what value they should be getting and what objectives you want to achieve by the end of the meeting. A main marker of this step's success is when you know everyone is viewing the way forward from the same point on the map.

Consistently Cultivating Trust

Look to another quality of the Change Agent as you move forward with the Revenue Equation Diagnostic. Keep in mind that it asks the participants to rate each question honestly. In an organization where things aren't functioning at their best, there may be hesitation by some members of the group to give honest answers. This is the first opportunity for the Change Agent to start cultivating trust.

The Change Agent needs to first remember that every team is different. While normally I have each person complete the diagnostic and then share with everyone, sometimes that process requires a few more steps to build a sufficient amount of trust. You might need a couple of introductory meetings, as a big group, smaller groups, one-on-ones, or all of those, before you get started.

When I am the Change Agent, and this is my first moment with the Improvement Team, and they don't know me yet, I spend a little time orienting them. First, I introduce myself and the work that I do, and as a way to generate interest and inspiration, I may ask them to think of their future state. What will it look like for them if the company improves? Will they be able to sell more, achieve sales targets, unlock bonuses, and make more money? Will they feel less stressed or happier at work? Will they get along better with their teammates? Will it be easier for them to get to all the things they need to do? Will they be able to help their customers better?

Depending on what I've seen ahead of time, I might also decide to split the sessions. For example, I might turn to the VP of sales and say, "Would it be okay if you stepped out of the meeting so we can give the team a little more space while I do this exercise with them?" Then the sales team will have a little bit more freedom to be honest without feeling pressured to give the answer they think their boss wants to hear. Just remember to talk with the VP first, so you have their buy-in and know that they understand the value of your work with the team.

THE PARKING LOT MODERATING TOOL

Once you are in a place where people are freely sharing their thoughts, you still need to moderate in a way that provides everyone with an opportunity to speak without making people feel ashamed or cut off. One method I use frequently is "the parking lot." It's a concept that allows people to be heard, get their ideas out, and feel validated without pulling the conversation away from its planned trajectory.

If I've started a meeting by presenting the intended topics, the way they'll be discussed, and the amount of time it will take, I'm already halfway there in terms of inspiring confidence and providing security. However, that doesn't mean other topics and ideas won't show up for people. If discussing something new is going to take us off course for more than a couple of minutes, I put it in the parking lot. If it's off topic, that doesn't mean it's not valuable; in fact, unexpected ideas can be incredibly insightful and can benefit all the participants in the future. I say, "Let's hold this thought in the parking lot while we process these other ideas, and then we'll come back to it."

If Tyrone, a United Events salesperson, has an idea that he's really excited about partway through a meeting and doesn't get to at least name it, he might get so involved with thinking about it that he cannot be present or get anything out of the meeting. If I conduct the meeting in the way I want to, there should be time at the end to come back to that parked idea. At that point, we'll be able to talk about it. If not, I might schedule a quick one-on-one with Tyrone so I can hear what he has to say and figure out how we might incorporate it into a future meeting or any follow-up work that the team might be doing between now and next time.

Seeking to Understand

Once I have everybody's trust and everyone knows the trajectory and purpose of this meeting, we can dive into deciphering responses to the Revenue Equation Diagnostic exercises. If people are willing to be honest, this assessment starts to show where the gaps in the Change Agent's understanding are. Now is the time for you to focus on your quest to understand each person's viewpoint and how their answers interact with one another's.

Sales Foundations

Foundations provide clarity on who your company is, the problems you solve, the value you create, the experience you create for your customers, your offerings, and how you communicate these concepts internally and externally. Participants are asked, on a scale of one to ten, one being the lowest, how well-defined and understood each of the following is within the organization.

1. **Problems We Solve:** The root problems that your organization solves for the customers

2. **Value Proposition:** The way you create value and deliver that value to your customers
3. **Key Differentiators:** The attributes that clearly separate you from the competition
4. **Offerings:** The products and/or services your company provides your customers
5. **Customer Experience Promise:** The defined experiences you want to create for your customers

Members of the Improvement Team may recognize the questions included in the Sales Foundations conversation as things they have read in an employee handbook or heard in a presentation that management showed them at one time or another.

Sales Foundations are a great starting place, because in one way or another, every person at the company is a salesperson. Each person, in their interactions with the outside world, represents the company. If they don't know what your company does and why, you're creating risks—and think how much more benefit you could create if everyone knew what you were about.

Sales Design

Sales Design defines who you sell to and how you provide them value. Participants are asked to rate on a scale of one to ten, one being the lowest, how well-defined and used each of the following is within your organization.

1. **Target Audience Organizations:** The types of organizations that purchase your offerings
2. **Target Audience Personas:** The hypothetical people best suited to purchase your offerings
3. **Sales Journey:** A series of steps buyers and sellers go through that represents the purchasing life cycle
4. **Campaigns:** Defined strategies and tactics to bring buyers into and through the sales funnel

Most sales and marketing people are pretty clear on their target audiences, scoring usually a seven or eight (unless this is an early-stage company still getting their bearings). The team more or less knows how they're supposed to show up for their customers. Where I have found it gets hairy is when I start talking about building personas for customers and customizing their individual sales journeys. When I ask whether they know their ideal customer's steps to buying, from learning about the product or service to deciding to purchase, team members often can't give me a clear yes.

After we evaluate how much thought they've put into it up until this point, I ask them to imagine a place where they could forecast their ideal customer's journey, starting with when they enter the funnel, to when they reach their decision to buy, and every step in between. I ask them to imagine how much that could help them sell and how they could make that process go more smoothly and quickly.

Then I remind them that what they are doing right now is taking them to that ultimate destination.

Sales Infrastructure

Refining your Sales Infrastructure creates accountability and efficiency and optimizes performance. Participants are asked to rate on a scale of one to ten, one being the lowest, how well-defined and used each of the following is within their organization.

1. **Roles and Responsibilities:** Defined ownership of activities within each stage of the sales funnel
2. **Sales Process:** Structured actions required to cultivate a prospect from lead stage to close
3. **Sales and Marketing Technology:** Tech used to increase sales funnel efficiency, organization, and effectiveness
4. **Sales Forecasting and KPIs:** Data used to evaluate team and sales funnel performance
5. **Performance Management:** Process to optimize the sales and

marketing of the organization

Sales Infrastructure is usually where understanding gets the shakiest. The diagnostic asks companies if they have organized and refined processes to manage their sales and whether they know who owns each step in the process.

Some people give fives or sixes in this category, but many score threes and fours. And that's okay—it's the reason we're defining this factor of your Revenue Equation in the first place. What people normally do to address infrastructural problems is just hire another person, but how is that person supposed to figure out their role in the company if they can't find their place? Is that person going to get the resources that they need to do the job and pick up the extra slack? If not, they're not going to be the savior you need them to be.

That's why the goal of the Revenue Equation is to put stabilization ahead of growth. The great part about setting priorities that way is that, even without trying a whole list of new tactics, it will feel like your organization is growing. Refining your infrastructure is the biggest step toward releasing trapped revenue without having to spend any more money, which you'll learn more about when you complete your Revenue Planner in chapter 9.

At this point, the Change Agent has set the table for all the participants and helped them envision a desired state. Getting there is doable if everyone knows where they are and can agree to give their best to reaching the destination. This is an opportunity to discover each team members' strengths and move that forward, and if you keep moving forward using the tools this book establishes, you will get there—improving all along the way.

ABC—Always Be...Committing

The Change Agent's responsibility is to cast a vision of the future that the company wants to see fulfilled after going through this work.

However, the vision of these desired states needs to be flexible enough to change according to unforeseen circumstances and the contribution of all participants. That's why it's important to constantly check in with your team. How you take their contributions, communicate them back to your team, and create alignment, clarity, and mutual agreement has a major impact on how much ownership they feel.

It's critical that you nourish that enthusiasm, especially since this process can run anywhere from three months to a year or more. People get tired. People fall off the wagon. People stop engaging when they're too busy; they start missing meetings and not doing the homework.

You can't just go on autopilot with this program. You need everyone to be committed, and if that means you have to put things on hold during a busy season and then come back refreshed, so be it. There isn't going to be true growth and improvement without enthusiastic engagement. But you'll only know the Improvement Team's state of mind if you check in with them.

Check in at the beginnings and ends of your meetings but also at other times. Check in when people seem tired or out of it. Check in when you hear someone has had a major success. Check in when you sense that people are becoming frustrated. Ask them if there's anything you can do to help them keep this work active in their life. Ask them if they still want what they originally said they did when they began this work. Remind the team of the future that they themselves have cast and that sticking to the path you're all on together is what is going to get them there. And do it often.

Chapter 5:
Who Are You?

Defining Your Sales Foundations

Imagine you're out having lunch with one of your friends. This friend is single, but he really wants to settle down and start a family. You have some reservations about this goal. You know that this friend barely knows what kind of person he even wants to date, much less marry.

Additionally, this friend is all over the place with how he even defines himself. Sometimes he's ultra-focused on his current career, sometimes he wants to throw it all away and move overseas, and sometimes he's convinced he should quit what he's doing and go back to school. You really value his friendship, but he doesn't really seem to be able to articulate who he is or what he wants in a partner.

Now imagine you've just been served drinks, and as you take a sip, your friend says, "I met this amazing woman last night, and we're getting married this Saturday! Wanna come?"

If you're anything like me, you might do a spit take all over him. That's bonkers, right?

I'm willing to bet that most people would be shocked if their friend, who barely knows who he is himself, decided to marry someone he also barely knows.

So, why do so many companies think that they can propose to a prospect they haven't taken the time to get to know?

If there's one thing I've seen almost every client of mine do, it's that. They try to immediately close a sale with a customer who has barely had a chance to get to know them, and vice versa. If they were to take that tactic in their dating lives, they'd probably land themselves on a reality TV show.

Working through the Revenue Equation means that you're not taking that slam-bang approach. You're moving slowly, with intentionality and an eye on the long game. You're establishing how you're going to be able to walk with the customer as they make the decision of whether or not to buy from your company.

But you can't even get to that point if you never introduce yourself properly. To do that, you first have to establish your identity as a company.

Agreeing on Your Sales Foundations

Remember the story I told you about that Improvement Team who compared their company to other brands? Remember how they all came up with contradictory answers?

That could be happening with your team right now, and you wouldn't even know it.

Your company is made up of many individuals, each of whom has their own conception of who your company is and who they are within it. If everyone can't agree on the problems you're solving, how they're solved, who you want to sell to, and how you're going to sell it, then there's no way to gauge how each person's contribution will work as part of the whole. The individual members of your team are just spinning around the universe in different directions instead of intentionally orbiting a planet. Sometimes they move in the same direction, and sometimes they don't. There's no plan or structure to it.

In chapter 8, we will discuss how to harness each team members' unique strengths and talents, but it's vital that the first thing you do is focus on the Revenue Equation for your organization. If you don't have a strong center of gravity that pulls all your people into orbit, you'll continue to operate without the intentionality you need.

Determining your company's Sales Foundations brings the organization into alignment on your company's core message and values and then moves you seamlessly toward a conversation about what is holding you back.

The Change Agent will be leading the Improvement Team members as you dive into these fundamentals. It's going to take some time, a secure space, and some prework. Specifically, there are a series of questions the team will be asked to fill out before the Change Agent brings them together. The goal of the meeting is to talk through everyone's answers, much the same way you compared the results of your Revenue Equation Diagnostic. This time, count on it taking more than one session.

Holding the Vision for Your Sales Foundations

Everyone is motivated to do their work by something internal. If we're talking about the founder, it might be that they started the company from scratch, and they take pride in it. For a salesperson, it might be that they need rent money. Just like everyone has their own internal motivators, they probably have their own ideas about the underlying foundations of the company and how those foundations benefit the customer.

When you, as the Change Agent, are working to keep everyone moving from start to finish, remember that you'll often be working with people who aren't necessarily used to this kind of collaborative, somewhat abstract process. They may never have stopped to consider their company's identity—what value they create, what their key differentiators are, and what problems they solve. This may even be true for founders.

Take Mark, for example, the founder of United Events. Mark was an AV kid in high school, and when he grew up, he made money running sound at a music venue. Eventually he took a steadier job at a hotel, where he'd help companies keep their conferences on track.

Then Mark got frustrated with his job and decided to start building his own company. Ten years later, he has a company doing $5 million in revenue a year and employing thirty-five people. Do you think Mark has spent a lot of time sitting around a boardroom table, talking about concepts like Sales Foundations of his company? Probably not.

Lots of SMBs are in this situation, especially ones that are family businesses. Employees are more likely to be a cousin's friend who is straight out of college, and the second-in-command might be the owner's thirty-year-old son-in-law. These younger or inexperienced people often have never had real mentorship on how to do these deep dives into the fundamentals of what they sell.

That brings us back to Mark, the founder who brought United Events from the ground up. He wanted to keep doing the work he loves finding audiovisual solutions, but instead he was trying to figure out how to stop leaking revenue, bring his team together, and build systems and processes doing the work of a chief operations officer. It was obvious that Mark was having exactly the struggles that I just described and that are so common to people who lead and run small and midsize companies.

I asked him, "Mark, do you feel like people don't listen to you in meetings? Do you feel like you can't move things forward or keep everyone focused?"

The answers were yes, yes, and yes. I told him that he was in luck because I had some tricks for him to keep things organized and on track, even though he lacked experience leading business development–oriented meetings. I started telling him about techniques to having these creative conversations without going completely off the rails. The first was the parking lot trick that I mentioned in chapter 4, and the others are the ones that I'm about to share with you.

What Phase Are You In?

In some people's minds, the connection between brainstorming, processing, and implementation is linear. First, they start with brainstorming, then move to processing the results of those brainstorms, and then put the results into action.

It might not be so linear in your head, however, especially if you have a more creative nature. It's certainly not that way for me. When I started leading group discussions, I would shift around these three phases faster than people could follow. They wouldn't know if I was brainstorming or processing or implementing, and I would lose my audience.

A lot of people have a different problem when going through these sessions, though—they gravitate toward one phase or another and approach every meeting from their preferred mindset. While someone like me might be jumping from brainstorming, to implementing, to processing, to implementing again, and then back to brainstorming, some people stay rooted in one place. My higgledy-piggledy approach meant that my meetings were a mess. People were leaving them mentally exhausted and unsure whether they should put anything we'd discussed into action or if they were just ideas.

Heavily left-brained project managers might want to jump straight to implementing. Some participants are more interested in processing ideas and will try to talk out everything in a brainstorming session as soon as it shows up. Meanwhile, you might get to the stage of figuring out how to implement a plan you've settled on, and the brainstormers just have one more idea that they wanted to get out there.

In a group setting, a structured and clearly defined approach really should be followed. That way, you're in line with the key Change Agent quality of holding the vision and keeping the entire team working from the same vantage point. Whether you are the Champion, the Change Agent, or another participant, mindfulness can keep you on track.

First, draw three columns on a whiteboard (or create those columns in a shared document, if you're conducting your work remotely), labeling them "brainstorming," "processing," and "implementing." As the facilitator of the meeting, you need to have that reminder for yourself, as well as for everyone who happens to be working with you.

Then, define the terms of whatever phase you're working within.

Brainstorming is just throwing out whatever idea shows up. It doesn't matter if it's the right idea or not. Anything goes. No one but the Change Agent needs to write anything down. This is a safe place for uncontrolled creativity.

Next is processing, where you decide which ideas people would like to pursue more deeply. Everyone agrees on a definition of the idea, discusses how it might hypothetically benefit the company, and figures out whether it makes sense to put into practice.

Then, once the team has a clear idea of what you'll do with these ideas, it's time to take the project management software out, set some timelines, and delegate roles and responsibilities to make it into a tangible plan. A lot of that kind of implementation happens as you complete the Sales Infrastructure factor of the Revenue Equation.

It's as simple as lining up that trajectory. Then everyone knows where they stand when it comes to their place during the meeting, how they can participate, and what is required of them.

Typically, each of us has a preference for one part of this work. If you're more structured and action-oriented, devoting enough time and energy to the brainstorming phase without plowing forward to processing and implementing might be your challenge. Whichever way you're inclined, you need to be able to identify your strongest and weakest of the three. That self-awareness allows the meeting to be more effective for everyone who is involved.

Always remember that the parking lot tool is there for you and is dynamite at helping people stay focused on whatever phase they're working in. If the project manager, for instance, starts talking about implementing one of the ideas the salesperson threw out during a brainstorm, you have an easy way to steer everyone back to where you're going. Acknowledge the project manager's input, thank them, and write it down or type it up so you can revisit it at the end of the meeting. When you do return to it, the PM will know that you really do value their input and aren't just paying lip service, and they will be encouraged to continue sharing thoughts.

Build and Maintain Trust by Using the Hat Trick

If you find yourself struggling to stay on topic or remain within whatever your least-favorite phase is, you might try a communication tool I call "the hat trick." It's a method I use to keep conversations on track, much like the parking lot, and one that I use in all parts of the Revenue Equation to solve problems and conflicts.

The hat trick is a method of tackling problems that puts you into whatever role is best for the task. We have a joke in my family that I act more like a big brother to the kids most of the time because we spend a lot of time having adventures and even being a little irresponsible. When it's time to get serious, though, I tell them that I've put on my Dad Hat. It helps my sons—and me—understand that it's time to be responsible.

If you have a bit of a friendly, casual relationship with members of the Improvement Team but you need to get down to business one day to implement some important initiative, you might need to let everyone know that you're wearing your VP of Sales Hat that day. When you tell your team that's the hat you're wearing, you're labeling something that might otherwise have caused major awkwardness. "I just need you to know that I might come across as short or impersonal, but I've got a roomful of people, and we need to make sure we cover everything in the next hour."

Preceding your actions with a description of what hat you're wearing helps participants understand what you are doing and why you are behaving in a certain way. Not only are they then able to mentally follow the work you're doing, they also aren't going to be worrying about whether you have suddenly stopped liking them. They now know that you're wearing your VP of Sales Hat, and that's why you have that "taking care of business" approach.

More often than not, the hat you are wearing as the Change Agent is one of some type of guide, fact finder, or facilitator. But remember, it's a hat, not a mask. It's another method you can use to show everyone which direction you'll be moving in that day. That's keeping the process transparent, not hidden.

When I'm trying to figure out where the inefficiencies are in a sales organization, I put on my Sherlock Holmes Hat. When I'm seeking to understand what a team member means when they're talking about a challenge they're having, I'm wearing my Investigative Reporter Hat. I like to ask the teams I work with to put on a Customer Hat when they're considering how to position themselves and their offerings in the most effective way possible.

This trick can really do wonders. It might have something to do with tapping into the kidlike nature inside each of us, the self who likes to play pretend, but regardless of whether my armchair psychology is correct, I get a lot of creative results from the people I work with when they're asked to step into a role like this.

Seek to Understand by Defining Your Terms

I can't overstate the importance of curiosity for the Change Agent, and that takes on a special dimension when working through a company's Sales Foundations. You need to be aware of body language, facial expressions, and the meaning behind what everyone at the table is saying, both individually and as a group.

I gave an example in chapter 2 of the time when I saw a display of groupthink around the word "partner." Everyone kept using that word, and I didn't think it meant what they thought it meant. The only way I could be sure, though, was by chipping a hole in that echo chamber and asking them to define what they were saying.

Sometimes you'll need to spell it out for the Improvement Team, like I did in that situation, but more often, if you ask enough questions, they'll come to these conclusions themselves.

Imagine I have United Event's Improvement Team all in one room; in this case, it's four salespeople along with a couple of people from marketing. As we review the questions in this section, I ask the group to tell me what they think makes their company different from others like it.

Rick in sales might say, "Well, we're different because we have really great audiovisual gear."

I say, "Okay, Rick thinks we have really great audiovisual gear," and I move on to the person next to him, who already is shaking his head, eyes slightly narrowed. "Tyrone, what do you think?"

"I don't actually think we have really great gear," Tyrone says. "We have okay gear, but there are other companies out there that have better gear than we do, and there's no way we can stay relevant on that level."

Now I have two people with different points of view, and so it's time to dig in. Before moving on to see what the next person says differentiates them, I need to go back to Rick.

"Rick, why do you say we have great audiovisual gear?" I ask. "How are you defining the word 'great'?" Before right now, Rick may have just held this belief without defining for himself what it meant. What "great" means to him is clearly not the same as what "great" means to Tyrone.

"Well, it's good quality and doesn't break down," Rick says. "We check it all the time to make sure it's working, and it's reliable."

I repeat back to him, "You're saying it's great gear because it's reliable, but you didn't say it's high-end or cutting-edge." When Rick agrees, I turn back to Tyrone. "Tyrone, how do you define, 'great gear'?"

"Oh, well, I define it as the most cutting-edge," Tyrone says. "It's the newest, the best, and has the most up-to-date feature set. It's expensive, and we don't have that." Around the table, the team members nod in agreement.

"So, Tyrone," I continue, "do we have reliable gear?" He agrees with that, and I address the next question to the rest of the group. "So, are we in agreement that we have reliable gear?" The team members all agree with that too.

Then Devon in marketing says, "That's not really a differentiator, though. Everybody has reliable gear."

Jackie, a third salesperson, says, "Well, not really. Everybody *thinks* they have reliable gear, but we have really reliable gear." I ask her what she means, and she continues, "I've worked at other companies, and they think they have reliable gear, but they don't quality check it when it comes back like we do. They don't have certified techs like we do, either."

Getting into defining terms gets people into this place where they're not just using the same buzzwords about their company that everyone else in their industry says. Because I asked questions when I saw these two different points of view between Rick and Tyrone, we got to Jackie's insight about what their gear's true differentiator is and why. To this company, "great" gear is reliable, less costly, and can be trusted to work consistently due to quality testing by certified technicians.

If I'm in an environment where the Improvement Team is providing new insights into the company's identity, I need to stay with each individual until they're absolutely clear on what they're saying. Only then should I move to the next. By my seeking to understand each of these individuals, we eventually came to a consensus as a group regarding the type of gear we have.

Defining your terms, especially within a discussion of Sales Foundations, is vital. In fact, I encourage the Change Agent to literally write down any recurring word they hear, and once it is explicitly defined, write that definition into your permanent Sales Foundations record. That way, when you are talking through your results, then encoding what it says as a guide for your team to refer to later, you won't just have a manual full of meaningless jargon.

Defining Who You Are as a Company

I'm now going through the questions that we ask during the course of establishing our Sales Foundations. Coming to an agreement on the following subjects allows each person on the team to unite behind consistent messaging when they present the company and its offerings to customers. That way, you don't have one salesperson out in the world telling people your company is like Costco and another telling them you're like the Ritz-Carlton. You'll be asking each team member for their input on the following topics.

1. Problems You Solve
2. Value Proposition
3. Key Differentiators
4. Offerings
5. Customer Experience Promise

In the last chapter, you had team members fill out their answers to the Revenue Equation Diagnostic quiz on their own, then bring their answers to the rest of the group. This time, you're using the prompts given here to guide your discussions.

Problems You Solve: What You Can Do for the Customer

You are in business because there are specific problems you solve. Revisiting these problems, and why you got into business to solve them, will provide insight into your Sales Foundations. You could even think of them as journaling prompts—all it takes is a little bit of thoughtfulness about what the sales organization does daily to come to a conclusion.

- Why did you get into business in the first place?
- What problems do you currently solve for your customers?
- What other problems would you like to solve for them?

Teams usually do pretty well in aligning on this topic, so it's a great one to start with. At the end of the discussion, we usually have a bulleted list compiled from everyone's answers. As the Change Agent, I then read through the list that we discussed, and generally agreed on, and group the responses under umbrella concepts. For example, here are a few overarching problems that United Events came up with.

Team Problems: Our experienced production professionals never miss a detail, collaborating with your team to achieve your outcomes with the least amount of stress possible (and having fun while we're at it).

Gear Problems: We know what gear will bring your vision to life and can readily access what you need while staying within your budget.

Expertise Problems: With thousands of events under our belts, we have a proven process to execute your vision flawlessly and right on schedule, with ready solutions for whatever unexpected problems might arise.

Value Proposition: The Value You Create for Your Customers

The previous question sets the stage for discussing creating value—when you solve someone's problem, you are inherently creating value for them too. Your value proposition represents the most important part of your company. When your value proposition is unclear or nonspecific, the result is confusion about your brand and the benefits you create, both inside of the organization and outside of it. Ultimately this confusion can lead to lost sales. Why would a customer buy from you if they're not sure what you're actually trying to sell them? Your value proposition should be so embedded in your daily communications and something that you can describe immediately and succinctly at a moment's notice.

As usual, I have each person share their own thoughts first. For this exercise, I ask them to write out their own understanding of what the company's value proposition is, defining any terms that come up along the way. Fortunately, when you have just finished creating a comprehensive list of the problems you solve for your customer, it follows that you'd be thinking about ways to solve them. When you're done going through everyone's answers, the

Change Agent can suggest an approximately twenty-five-word and hundred-word summary.

EXAMPLE OF 25-WORD VALUE PROPOSITION

United Events is an event production company that works side by side with our customers to plan and execute events that exceed expectations, run flawlessly, and stay on schedule.

EXAMPLE OF 100-WORD VALUE PROPOSITION

United Events works side by side with agencies, corporations, associations, and nonprofit event organizers, taking your vision from idea to execution, flawlessly, and right on schedule. United Events lets companies focus on their expertise while applying our own expertise to produce events that exceed expectations and fully engage audiences.

Our team of experienced professionals has produced thousands of events and can access the right technologies and resources to craft any solution. We follow a proven process, producing successful results time and time again, and will collaborate with your team to achieve exceptional outcomes and keep your stress levels low.

Key Differentiators: The Things That Set You Apart

It's true that there are probably plenty of companies doing the same thing that you do, but definitely not in the exact same way. Just like everyone is unique, there's a certain nameless quality that makes each company different. Except, guess what? It won't be nameless for long—because you and the team are about to name it. Key differentiators should be unique, quantifiable, and defendable, and they should answer the question:

Why should someone purchase the product or service from you instead of from any of the other alternatives in the marketplace?

A follow-up question I use that might help get the brain synapses firing is **Why have customers bought from you in the past?**

By the way, you need to be especially careful defining your terms here. The "great audiovisual gear" misunderstanding that I described earlier in the chapter arose from the discussion of key differentiators.

Offerings: How You Deliver Value

The entrepreneurial bug bit my sons while we were on the last stretch of a road trip, and they informed me of their plan to start a lawn care business—Brothers Mowing Service.

Barely concealing my pride (I myself had lawn mowing service from junior high through much of college), I put on my Sales Consultant Hat. "So, what are you going to say if you knock on a neighbor's door and someone answers?"

My older son answered, "Hi there, I'm Sam, and my brother and I live up the street. Would you like us to mow your lawn this weekend?"

"Nice to meet you, Sam," I said, getting into character. "How much do you charge?"

My younger son, Morgan, jumped in, "We'll give you the best deal in town!"

Aha! Time to teach my favorite lesson. "Well, Morgan, I don't recommend that you sell on price. Let's think about what else we might do." I started to paint a picture of a front yard with a swing set, a soccer ball, and—naturally—an overgrown lawn. When Dad opens the door, you can hear the kids shouting in the background.

I could tell they were thinking hard about what I was getting at. "Do you think that he might be excited if he didn't have to spend a couple of hours on a Saturday morning mowing his lawn? Maybe he could be bringing his kids to soccer practice or even having a cup of coffee and reading the newspaper." (A man can dream, right?)

Their eyes lit up. They got it. "We're gonna be rich!" Morgan yelled. And that weekend they started raking it in.

Flash-forward—it's Take Our Daughters and Sons to Work Day, and Sam is sitting in on a brainstorming session that I'm leading with the CEO and Improvement Team in attendance. I had asked everyone to bring in ideas for boosting revenue, and we went around the room to get everyone's answers, ending with the CEO.

When it was his turn, the CEO excitedly said, "Let's offer deep discounts during the months when we don't usually have much business."

I saw Sam's eyes widen, and he raised his hand. From my place at the whiteboard, I looked at the CEO for permission. He smiled and nodded, and I told my twelve-year-old son, founding partner at Brothers Mowing Service, to go ahead and give his input.

"Dad, I thought you said we should never sell on price."

The sales team burst out laughing, and luckily, so did the CEO. And it turned out, Sam had broken the tension that the marketing and sales team had been holding. They all wanted to say it, but he had done it for them.

Offerings are the products and services your company provides its customers. In this discussion, you're going to be asked to dig deeper and really think about what your offerings are, particularly in terms of how they might look to prospects. In fact, you should probably ask your Improvement Team to dust off their Customer Hats for this one.

Offerings are built from your value proposition and differentiator and are aligned to the needs, interests, and wants of your customers. The more that your purpose is aligned with theirs, the better; otherwise, they might not see all the benefits that your offering can bring them. You need to consider who your target audience is, how what you're offering will address their needs, and how you can present that to them in the course of their sales journey (which we will cover in detail in the next chapter).

It's essential to constantly revisit your offerings to ensure they're bringing you the highest probability of success. In fact, it's something that I usually recommend people look at first when they really need a quick win (see chapter 9 for details).

Can you imagine how a 5–20 percent increase in the number of leads would affect your business? Or if 25–50 percent of your leads were more qualified when they began their interaction with your sales team? The more alignment you can create and the more clarity your team has, the more efficient your sales and marketing activities will be. You will bring in more leads, the leads will be more qualified, and the length of your sales cycle will decrease. Clarity and alignment of offerings, together, is one of those levers that can really set your organization up for success.

GET YOUR OFFERINGS STRAIGHT

When you work with your team to get clarity and alignment on your offerings, use these jumping-off points to shape the conversation.

1. Start by listing all your offerings—what they are called and what they do. You might consider using a table like this one.

Offering—What It's Called	Description—What It Does

2. List all the outcomes associated with each offering. Take your time here and be super thorough. Dig deeper into the outcomes your offerings create. This both provides great introspection as well as reminds the Improvement Team how your customers receive value. I find that this table helps guide that discussion.

Offering	Outcome	Why the Outcome Is Important to Our Customers

3. Why is your offering better than your competitor's?

Customer Experience Promise: What It Is Like to Work with You

The experiences you create for your customers come from the interactions they have with you and your team. Creating a single customer experience promise defines the experiences you want to create and provides a guiding star to how everyone in your organization interacts with the people you serve.

We're dealing with more than solving day-to-day, concrete problems in this section. We're talking about human interaction, and therefore the team members have to go through a deeper brainstorming process, both on their own and when you come together as a team to discuss answers.

I start out by having them generate a list of keywords and phrases that they think represent the impression they want their customers to have of their company. Examples include:

- Dependable
- Delightful
- Hardworking
- Resourceful

- Diligent
- Above and beyond
- Simple
- Persistent

Once they've written out their keywords and phrases, they choose three or four that they think reflect the company the best. You then go through the process of defining what these qualities truly mean to each person again and narrow down to the top three or four key words and phrases for the company. For example:

- **Dependable:** Able to be relied on as honest or truthful
- **Delightful:** Causing delight, highly pleasing, or fun
- **Simple:** Easily understood or done; presenting no difficulty

You won't stop at collecting and defining these words, however. Each team member will arrive with their own version of the customer experience promise using the words they chose in the prior section. These are building blocks to cocreate the promise; no single person should expect to be chosen as the "winner." Your customer experience promise, with everyone's input, might look like this:

Working with our company is a dynamic and enjoyable experience with dependable results. Our team is experienced, knowledgeable, and delightful to work with. You'll become a devoted fan when you witness our dedication to your best possible outcome and how we apply our experience pulling off hundreds of events to keep yours simple and running smoothly.

Your Foundational Messaging

Now that you've defined your terms—e.g., what "great gear" *really* means—and have determined what unique value you can offer to solve your customer's problems, it's time to bring everything together. New customers typically move through the sales funnel through a series of decisions. These decisions are based on their understanding of your company, your solutions, and the experiences you create for your customers. And naturally, your guidance as a sales organization is vital to keep them on the right track.

Your foundational messaging creates a coherent narrative, and you will be able to walk each customer through it as they consider whether they should buy from you. This narrative will be a great resource for you and all the members of your team to use when you need to answer questions. It's also a great way to screen customers who might not be a good fit. Remember, the more aligned everyone is, the more successful your company will be.

For instance, think about what each salesperson in the room likes to do and ask them to imagine themselves in a scenario where they'd meet someone who either is or can connect you with your ideal customer. I like to run a bit of a simulation, depending on what I know about the individual salesperson's interests to generate this list of questions and answers.

For instance, I know that Rick at United Events likes to play tennis on the weekends, and I asked him to imagine that he meets up with someone who works at a local agency that puts on a yearly conference. After telling him to put on his Customer Hat, I asked him to imagine wrapping up a tennis match and then grabbing a beer with the person.

I said to Rick, "You know that this person might be able to introduce you to people at his company who are in charge of conferences, training workshops, or other events that might be good for United Events. What questions do you think he'd ask, and how would you answer them?"

Asking him to imagine himself in a familiar scenario and then putting on his Customer Hat helped Rick get into this headspace, but it was all the work that we'd done together that helped him with both the questions and the answers.

Who is your company, and what do they do?

How does your company create value?

What type of results do your customers get?

What is it like to work with your company?

What are the next steps if we do decide to work together?

You have the language all set out to use to guide these conversations. Now, it's just a matter of practice. You can customize this scenario for the person who goes to lots of networking events, the person who is part of the local bowling league, the person who volunteers at a dog rescue. Whatever social or business setting your salespeople can picture themselves in is a great starting place for practicing your Sales Foundations.

The ideas you've been discussing all along will start to take shape in a conversational form, and then you can bring everyone together to hone and record the language you've come up with. You'll also be confident that every person in the room has a handle on a consistent, agreed upon way to represent your company.

Having all this messaging for every step in the process will help you court your customers, from the first meeting, through their evaluative process, and to finally closing the sale. If you have a clear understanding of who your company really is, you're that much closer to building a true relationship before anyone is pushed into a commitment that they may or may not be ready for. You'll be spared the enormous risk of rejection (or worse, a terrible match) that comes with proposing to someone you just met.

Chapter 6:
Who Are You Selling To?

Designing Your Customer's Sales Journey

By now, the Improvement Team of your sales organization will have created a guidebook to your company's Sales Foundations based on the work you did in the last chapter. If you're the Change Agent, and you've truly been seeking to understand the company's current state, you will have these foundations front of mind, along with the wants and needs of the Decision Makers at your company. That means when you dive into the real operations of your sales organization, you're going to be more likely than anyone else to see where the cracks are.

Sometimes when I interview a member of the Improvement Team, I can tell right away what actions of theirs will make the Decision Makers and other contributors at the company happy and what will make them need to crack open a bottle of antacids. The more stomachache-inducing behaviors tend to be things like underselling and overpromising deliverables. Salespeople usually do these things because they're miscommunicating what value their offering can really bring to customers. I saw this phenomenon with Rick at United Events.

Rick is one of the nicest salespeople I've ever met, but he was so nice that he was timid about going for customers who would bring in major revenue. Rick's personality was more in line with that of an account manager or customer service rep, but in his role, he had responsibility for both managing a book of business and developing new accounts. The way he saw it, talking about money put him at risk of conflict and in danger of not being seen as a friend.

Instead of swinging for the fences with the leads he was provided, he'd contact small hotels to see if they needed a partner who would support their events when they had them. These were hotels that were too small to have an in-house audiovisual team and might have a few small gatherings a year that needed basic audiovisual equipment and maybe a couple thousand dollars' worth of work. Rick would spend a lot of time building up these relationships and always going the extra mile to be seen as their partner—driving extra gear down to where they were, setting things up himself, and throwing in freebies. Because he was such a nice guy, these venues had nothing but nice things to say about him…to other small venues. That meant he stayed within a small community of low-revenue customers, providing solutions that were not the focus of the company.

Rick's desire to avoid conflict led him to consistently get, and stick with, accounts that didn't fit United Events' Sales Foundations. Ironically, that ended up generating a triangle of conflict between himself and the company's Sales Foundations, between himself and the customer, and between his customer and the company. He was creating more and more of what he wanted the least.

A fellow salesperson at United Events, Jackie, had a little more confidence in her approach. She welcomed the opportunity to put herself out there, to learn about her leads and engage in discovery conversations. She was willing to be more assertive when communicating the company's values to their customers. She was always up-front and transparent with leads from the beginning, saying, "We're not the lowest price in town, but we're great at what we do." If Jackie threw in a freebie, she'd make sure the customer knew that they'd need to make room in their budget to pay for it next time. She'd go on to place herself in the role of a trusted advisor for the customers, to the point that they wouldn't blink when she'd quote them a price. Because of her clear communication of the company's Sales Foundations, they would understand that what she was offering would solve their problems. As a result, Jackie's sales numbers and profit margin were consistent and strong.

With the sales projections for the next year set pretty high, Mark was worried about Rick's habit of working with small venues, and he told me as much.

"But if he were making his sales goal, would you care about who his customers were?" I asked.

"No, but I really don't think he's doing the margins we want with the kinds of places he's been working with," Mark said.

"Well, what has he done historically?"

Mark paused. "I don't know," he said. "I haven't looked."

Aha. Another misalignment uncovered.

While Rick was selling in a way that was out of alignment with United Events' Sales Foundations, he also wasn't being managed in a way that was going to help keep him focused on those foundations, or on the kind of customers that the company wanted to work with. If Decision Makers expect their salespeople to all move toward the same goal together, they need to guide them into committing and recommitting to their shared values—and to the type of customer they're targeting.

Some companies have an easier time figuring out their ideal customer, especially if they sell products that only serve a specific purpose. With custom work, though, where highly competitive solution-selling and varied prices are the norm, it can be more difficult to pin down. Unless you are Costco, you probably shouldn't be selling based on price. You need to sell based on value, and you need to sell to customers who will understand what value you truly offer.

As you continue the process of balancing your company's Revenue Equation, you'll be looking at the gears and component parts of the company in greater detail: from team performance as a whole, down to individual sales performance, and how those performances affect profit margin and longevity. Only that way can you connect the dots between what you've all just agreed upon and what those values look like in action. If you're the Change Agent, plan on having some one-on-ones with each salesperson about the customers they work with.

Not every customer who comes your way is the right fit. Some of them can even lose you money, and taking on just anyone's business can lead you to using up time that could have been better spent cultivating a relationship and working with a customer who pays better and whom you enjoy working with more. When you have several salespeople with different books of business, coming together to examine your pool of customers will be vital to you being able to identify your sales leaks and wasted opportunities.

Determining Sales Design means asking your Improvement Team to get together and take very honest looks at their customers and then identify who are great fits, good fits, and poor fits for your company. In this chapter, we explore the criteria that sales organizations can use to determine the market segments you most want to work with, identify target audience personas, and understand the 5-Step Sales Journey that represents the path a person will go through when they're deciding whether to purchase from you.

Sort Your Customers by Performance

Believe it or not, it is possible to turn sorting your ideal customers into a quantifiable process. Just like you begin balancing your Revenue Equation by determining your high-level Sales Foundations, you'll start identifying your ideal customers from a ten-thousand-foot view. You start with broad strokes by figuring out what type of companies you like to work with best, then narrow your vision to the more nuanced decisions of the individual companies themselves.

Pick Your Favorite Buckets

Start at the most basic level by listing all your customers' market segments and separating them into "buckets" accordingly. For United

Events, those market segments include nonprofits, corporations, associations, and agency partners. These wider classifications will likely catch each of your customers. You can always create a miscellaneous bucket for the ones who don't quite fit in any of the other categories.

Once you have them split into different market segments, you create new category filters within these buckets you've laid out. Creating subcategories isn't based on some rigid structure but on the Improvement Team's experience of working with each company. When you take a step back and look at your list of customers, their natural similarities will show up.

Some other variables might include:

- Industry or sector that they're in (e.g., biotech, SaaS, professional services)
- Company demographics (e.g., number of employees, territory covered, type of customer they serve)
- Volume and frequency of contact with you
- Number of transactions per year
- Value of each transaction (revenue and margin)
- How they buy (Based on value? Based on price? Based on discounting?)

Breaking these into categories and subcategories will make you and the Improvement Team aware of trends both for the sales organization overall and for the salespeople individually. For example, an event production company like United Events might mainly serve national nonprofits who buy based on budget, corporations with annual sales conferences that buy on creative and value-producing ideas, and a mixed bag of agencies—some of whom buy based on price and others who base their decisions more on value, expertise, and relationships.

If you have a lot of different customers to consider, cut the list down to no more than ten categories, but try to target no more than seven. This will enable you to see big-picture trends and help you and your Improvement Team stay focused.

Find the Best of the Bunch

It's obviously difficult to apply a quantitative process to a customer's quality. After all, how do you assign a score to a relationship? When it comes to identifying your best customers, however, making a measured judgment of each of them can help you get out of your revenue slump. That's because you'll be able to analyze what characteristics they have that you like and don't like, then use those characteristics to determine where to direct your sales and marketing efforts in the future. The goal of the Sales Design phase of the Revenue Equation is to have a higher-level picture of the kind of customers you want your sales organization to focus on.

My recommendation is to give each customer a rating from one to ten under the following three criteria: financial profitability, headache, and enjoyment. Under each of these, I've included several considerations that will affect your rating process.

FINANCIAL PROFITABILITY

Is the return on investment (ROI) on this customer worth your sales organization's time? Consider:

- Percent revenue, or how much money they bring into the company, and what percentage of your company's yearly revenue they account for
- Profit margin, or your net income from that customer per transaction or overall
- Average number of transactions per year
- How long the customer has worked with you and how often you do business with them
- Current lifetime value and forecasted lifetime value

HEADACHE

Does this customer suck the energy out of you and your people? Consider:

- How the delivery team and other customer service reps respond when asked about this customer
- How often the customer makes special requests, requires non-standard solutions, or demands special accommodations
- Whether they communicate regularly (or too often)
- Whether they need extra hand-holding
- Whether they treat members of the team respectfully

ENJOYMENT

If your team only worked with their favorite type of customer, would this account make the cut? Consider:

- How the customer reflects back to your organization by giving referrals, testimonials, or offering to be subjects of case studies
- Whether you are aligned with your customer's mission/vision
- Their level of openness to feedback or advice
- How much fun you have working with them and whether you could see hanging out with them outside of work
- If money were no object, whether you would choose to work with them over another customer

There might be some customers you love, who score high in every category, and you don't need to puzzle over them. While the "headache" and "enjoyment" categories might be subjective for each person giving a rating, questions having to do with margin and revenue can be answered by looking at the hard data. The most constructive conversations happen when both qualitative and quantitative attributes are taken into account.

To choose which of these three categories matters to you the most, you'll ask what your sales organization is aiming for and consider the company's goals and Sales Foundations. Are you part of a family business where work-life balance is a high priority? You might prioritize high enjoyment and low headache and be willing to take less financially profitable customers. Are you hoping to bring in as much revenue as possible and sell this company in three years? Then you might decide to keep taking the headache customers who pay a lot of money.

While your first reaction might be that nobody should take on a customer who causes major headaches, there might be factors that make some companies not mind it so much. If a customer is offering a huge amount of money, for instance, and your company is on the edge of financial collapse, the level of enjoyment won't be at the top of the list. The customer might be a major headache, but at the end of the day, you want a big valuation to bring yourselves back to a safe place again. A company with these goals might be willing to go for high profitability, high headache, and low satisfaction, at least for the moment.

Conversely, you might turn down some pretty lucrative customers due to your values, your financial comfort level, and to be real, your tolerance for nonsense. If you've been in business long enough, you know that there are people out there who truly act like movie villains in the way that they run their companies, including in the way they communicate with both their own internal team and the world outside. Even if these villainous types are offering millions of dollars, many business owners aren't willing to put up with that kind of headache-inducing behavior.

If your company prioritizes long-term relationships with customers and also needs to meet certain revenue requirements, there might be a more complicated balance between each of these qualities. Whereas with your Sales Foundations tiebreakers are usually based solely on a Decision Maker's priorities, with Sales Design, you have data. The numbers don't lie when it comes to profitability, and using the parameters we just discussed, people will be able to assign numbers to these more hard-to-pin-down characteristics. Ultimately, a Decision Maker can overrule any conclusion, but data can help make these decisions easier and more evidence based.

Once you've categorized your customers, determined how your priorities are weighted, then quantified the qualities of each customer, you'll be much more focused than before. You have one group of customers who are intense and sometimes difficult to work with yet bring in big numbers. You have another group of customers who are a delight but who don't have the big budgets you really need. Then, right there in the middle, is the customer you have a relatively good time working with and who pays you an amount of money that helps keep your business sustainable—even thriving. They may not necessarily be the most profitable or the most enjoyable, but they hit the sweet spot where, all in all, you'd love to have another ten customers like them.

If you are the Change Agent, once each customer has been rated and you have an idea of which ones are best (and worst) for your company, have everyone write their reasons for why they do or do not like working with that customer. You'll use these notes to help you to better identify where future customers fit and to do the next exercise—completing your target audience personas.

Leading Drama-Free Sales Design Discussions

While Sales Foundations basically reveal the origins and unconscious drivers of your business, things that you could argue have been a part of the company all along, the Sales Design phase of the Revenue Equation is where growing pains will really kick in. The exercises can often reveal where your Improvement Team will need to change their habits and possibly alter their existing customer relationships.

At this point, you need to remind yourself, as well as the Decision Makers in the room, to take a deep breath and be patient. You're making progress, yes, but it's still a slow and deliberate process rather than a magic bullet. The vision of change can be big, but the journey there must be incremental.

In small businesses, and especially family businesses, internal relationships are everything. To have a Decision Maker come in and demand abrupt changes is not only annoying, like it might be in a larger corporate setting, but it can actually hurt. In the case of the SaaS company I discussed in chapter 3, the CEO's resistance to change kept them all from the sort of transformation they'd been hoping to achieve. The opposite behavior—a desire to take the wheel and turn it hard in one direction or another—can damage trust between Improvement Team members and any other contributors who are affected by it.

If you are the Change Agent, remember that you are aligned with the company Decision Makers whether you are one or not. It doesn't do much good for you to push salespeople too far beyond their comfort zones, and that means you, the Champion, and any other Decision Makers need to have a plan to approach behavioral change in your salespeople with care. To suddenly ask them to make a major change—for instance, to drop a customer they have a long-term relationship with—is going to cause them too much anxiety, and it's probably not going to work.

Let's go back to Rick and the triangle of conflict he created because of the small hotel customers he'd been pursuing.

The company owner, Mark, gave me the go-ahead to work with Rick on discussing how his current sales aligned with his and United Events' sales goals. I knew better than to dictate to Rick that he make a seismic change. When we sat down for our one-on-one, I was honest, and my mission was to seek to understand his own attitude toward his approach to selling.

It turned out that Rick was just as frustrated as Mark was. He was unhappy with his numbers, but he didn't know what to do to get out of the hamster wheel he was stuck inside. He was happy to let me help him review his transactions to search where he had trapped revenue. Since he had been part of the Improvement Team's establishment of Sales Foundations, he started to see more of the areas where he was not demonstrating the company's value—where he was comping pricey equipment, where he wasn't charging for change orders, where he was providing his time and deep expertise at no cost.

It was now clear to Rick where his misalignments were and that it was time for him to move toward customers who would pay for all of the company's labor, knowledge, and resources. Rick's is a common problem, and most of the time these kinds of problems can be prevented with clear target audience personas.

When a Change Agent sits down and really listens and holds space for a salesperson like Rick, often that salesperson comes to see what needs to be done on their own. Then they're ready for the next step—determining which path forward is better for them and for the entire sales organization.

Target Audience Personas and the 5-Step Sales Journey

You may have heard of the buyer's journey—the process a potential buyer goes through from awareness of a solution, through evaluating their options, and finally to purchasing. I see that as only half of the story. If the buyer's journey is to mean anything to a sales organization, it must be recognized as running parallel to what actions sales and marketing take to meet them where they are. Only when the seller understands where the buyer is at every stage of their journey, with all the considerations and concerns that go along with someone in their place, will salespeople be able to do their jobs effectively.

Now that you have a better idea of the type of business you're going for based on those more concrete qualities, you're going to use them to build target audience personas. These are semifictional representations of your ideal customers based on the real data you just finished collecting about your existing customers. I normally ask a company to draw up three different personas of the customers they believe they will encounter the most and then have them anticipate and document each one's journey.

If I were to ask you to give a speech, your first question, even before you asked about the topic, would probably be about who you'd be giving it to. Who you are delivering a speech or presentation to affects the issues you emphasize, the needs you try to fill, and even the jokes you make. Forgetting where you are and who you are talking to can start a relationship with your audience off on the wrong foot and even be embarrassing or damaging.

Ever been to a concert where the band forgets what city they're in? It's the same thing when you're developing a plan to sell to your customers—you have to really know who that customer is in the first place. Otherwise, it's like you're walking onstage in Cleveland and yelling, "What's up, Detroit!"

The first thing that is important to state is that the persona you are creating is heavily tied to the type of business and position they're in. You can't take your marketing agency manager persona and plop them onto the board of a university alumni foundation. That's why you need to make sure you don't skip the first step in the chapter, where you categorize the types of businesses you want to work with.

After you've identified these categories, it's time to create your persona, then identify the checkpoints they'll pass through on their journey from their current state to buying from your company. By understanding the characteristics of each target audience persona and the five steps of their specific sales journeys, sales and marketing will improve the effectiveness of communication between your company and your target audiences. This improved communication creates higher degrees of alignment, provides more opportunities for engagement, and enables sales to more successfully guide leads through your funnel to closing the sale. These tools for engagement will take the form of content and talking points created for each step in the process, which I discuss later.

Sometimes when I ask the teams I work with what a good customer looks like, they get kind of stuck. Sometimes one of the Improvement Team members will only be able to answer, "Someone who pays on time."

I encourage you, if you are the Change Agent, to get the team into the right mindset for imagining their customer's state by having them envision a particular situation that customer might experience in real life. I ask them to think about meeting one of their target audience personas on a cross-country flight and how they would have an appropriate conversation to learn more about them. What might they say when the team member asks them about their work and life?

The Change Agent has been seeking to understand what the Improvement Team is going through and what they're trying to communicate and accomplish. Now, it's their turn to seek to understand the people they will be selling to and be able to walk with them through each of the following steps.

The 5-Step Sales Journey

For United Events, one of their biggest market-sector buckets was nonprofits. These organizations contacted them for help with putting on fundraisers, usually needing creative solutions to run live and silent auctions, dinners, presentations, and performances, all on a carefully quantified budget. To create an image of who that was, the Improvement Team created the persona of Nonprofit Nancy. Let's pretend we're sitting next to Nancy on a cross-country flight, get to know a little bit more about her, and then look at the 5-Step Sales Journey through her eyes.

Create a Target Audience Persona

First, you identify some basic biographical information about Nancy, starting with her personal demographics.

PRIMARY JOB TITLE

Director of Fundraising

ADDITIONAL TITLES

- Marketing Director
- Director of Communications
- Event Manager
- Entertainment Director

30s–50s

Woman

GENERAL CHARACTERISTICS

Nonprofit Nancy is a driven philanthropist who likes to be prepared; that's why she starts planning events up to eighteen months in advance. Since she spends most of her time raising money and organizing, sometimes she's a little uncertain about production and running events in general. This may not actually be her fulltime job, but what she does is very, very important to her. She is hands-off at times but is involved with managing multiple other details and people who are part of the event.

JOB ROLES AND RESPONSIBILITIES

Nancy has a lot of other things to worry about aside from production, particularly keeping her board of directors happy and raising money. She is busy dealing with performers, silent auctions, speakers, and sponsors. For her, it's a high-stakes, high-pressure game, and her eyes are on the outcome.

Step 1: The Customer's Current State

This is where you define where your target audience persona is right now, before they know anything about you and your company. Their current state doesn't have to be a complete disaster; in fact, it doesn't need to be negative at all, just a simple snapshot of their daily life. Knowing where they're coming from will help you better envision their desired state and how we might help them get there. Get to know your buyer by thinking through where they are under the following conditions.

TYPICAL WORKDAY

Now that Nancy is sitting next to you, it's natural to ask about the daily operations of her professional life. Here, you explore the idea of what a "normal day at the office" looks like for Nancy, as well as how that impacts her personal life.

It might be that Nonprofit Nancy only works at the nonprofit part-time due to budget constraints. Most of that time is spent trying to organize events, so she always has a phone to her ear and a spreadsheet in front of her. Maybe she works from home and also has a family to take care of, so she has a lot of responsibilities to juggle.

WORKING ENVIRONMENT

You now ask Nancy how she feels about the environment where she works. Is it high-pressure? Is it laid-back? Is she doing something she loves with people she loves?

In this case, Nancy loves being part of a team and community who are helping children, and she is good at raising money. She loves being in the nonprofit world. However, Nancy does experience uncertainty on a daily basis, as she figures out how to keep all the balls that she's juggling in the air, dealing with both donors and logistical details.

DAILY EXPERIENCE

You're going to think now of what experiences have an impact on how Nancy does her work. Nancy tells you that she is extremely organized—she has to be in order to organize events and make sure the donors' every need is attended to—and that she's following the guidelines set out by her board. The level of urgency she experiences has to do with how close to an event the nonprofit is and anything that may be happening in the world that requires them to raise more money for their cause.

Step 2: The Customer's Challenges

This is where you explore the negative aspects of what your customers are going through. While you should be thinking about how that relates to your industry and the solution you provide, you need to view it in the context of everything you just learned about your target audience persona's current state.

PROBLEMS

This is where you dig into the challenges that keep Nancy awake at night. Because of the many responsibilities she has, she has a lot to worry about. She is holding together every part of the event, and she doesn't have time to become an expert in every aspect. She can't be in several places at once, but with all the people she needs to impress, she sometimes feels like she is expected to be.

FAILURE

The Improvement Team of United Events needs to be able to anticipate what could go wrong in Nancy's line of work. What would be a disastrous situation for her? Under what circumstances would she consider herself or her work a failure?

With a nonprofit fundraiser, failure to raise money or to please the attendees and her board is a constant concern. There are so many moving parts that she's afraid of all the potential for things to go wrong. A speaker might get sick at the last minute, or more than one volunteer might be a no-show. What if the lights or the mic system goes out? What if the food isn't good? What if the donors aren't impressed and decide to give money to other organizations? What if nobody bids on the auction items?

You get it. If you get Nancy started on what could go wrong with her job, she's going to be able to talk for a long time.

STRESS

Now that you know the stakes for your customer, how can you identify what really stresses them out and makes them frustrated? Since all eyes are on Nancy, she gets worried when she doesn't understand how something works. She needs to know all the possible sticking points and what the consequences will be if something—or someone—isn't where it should be. However, if she's in an unfamiliar situation, she needs help to get her bearings. When people aren't helping her bring different elements together, she can become very stressed.

Step 3: The Customer's Desired State

Now that we've explored the customer's anxieties, it's time to turn them upside down and start getting optimistic! Let's envision Nancy's best-case scenario.

WAVE THE MAGIC WAND

If Nancy had a fairy godmother, what could they make her future state look like? Wave the magic wand and envision the perfect solution to Nancy's problem, the perfect outcome for the thing that has been on her mind. You should be able to paint as perfect a picture as you can. Really think big! Include the things you think are impossible or unlikely.

People tend to regulate themselves when they're asked what they truly want, but when you use the magic wand tool, you're removing the barrier of reality. This lets your persona tap into their greatest wishes for their future state and, in turn, lets your Improvement Team generate more creative ideas.

NANCY'S ESSENTIAL NEEDS

Needs are non-negotiables for your target audience persona. Not having these essentials means failure. On a car, these wouldn't just be the brakes and seat belts; they would also be the third row of seats if you have kids or the roof rack if you're a frequent surfer. Those last two features might not be necessary for every single person, but for some, not having them would be a failure.

Nancy has thrown events before, and her list of needs has grown over time, possibly because she's had to learn the hard way. Maybe she's had an event where there weren't enough seats, and when they brought chairs in at the last minute, the guests in the back couldn't see or hear what was going on at the front of the room. Baseline need? Everyone needs to be able to see and hear, no matter where they are in the room, and everyone needs somewhere to sit. Just like a family of six needs another row of seats in their van, for Nancy, planning for the unexpected isn't just a luxury—it is a necessity.

WHAT ELSE DOES SHE WANT?

You know what Nancy needs now. So, when you wave the magic wand, what else would she want to have for this event?

Wants are the things that Nancy would love to have but could do without if it's not in the budget. They're the things that exceed her baseline expectations and bring her that much closer to the vision created by the wave of your magic wand. Nancy needs a way to display the sponsors' names. She wants that way to be impressive—perhaps with their logos projected up on the wall of the venue. She needs everyone to see and hear everything, but she wants to have an extra screen and projector on top of the two that she had last year.

Also, don't forget to think about what she wishes her own experience for the event could be. For Nancy, the perfect event might mean she can sit down with her husband and enjoy the fruits of her hard work, rather than pacing up and down the back of the ballroom to see where something might go wrong. Her nonprofit would raise more money than ever before, and at the end of the night, everyone—especially her biggest donors—would thank her for putting on a perfect event.

Step 4: Solutions for the Customer

So, you think you can get Nancy to that fairy-tale ending—or at least pretty close. You're going to need to generate a list of solutions that are available to Nancy. Here's the catch, though. You are not the only person who can give her a positive outcome. That's why you have to have knowledge of everything that Nancy might be considering as a solution to her problem.

OPTIONS

Since Nancy is considering her options, you need to as well. And that means you need to think about every option available to her, not just what you offer. You need to know what solutions your competitors offer too, because she's going to be measuring you against them.

Nancy might be working for the nonprofit arm of an organization, and that might mean she has the option of using that corporation's in-house audiovisual team. She might also be considering just using the audiovisual team at the venue where the event will take place in addition to you, a third-party events production company.

You can think about other event production companies, but then you might go a few steps beyond that. For example, what if Nancy is able to reach that end state of raising more money than ever by not having a live event at all? What if she has a hugely successful virtual auction? What if she's able to reach it by doing a focused campaign targeting their best donors? Be as imaginative as possible.

CONSIDERATIONS

Now that you've named as many options for Nancy as you can, it's time for you to think about what other things she needs to consider as she puts the event together. Everyone needs somewhere to live, but not everyone needs a third bedroom in their house. If you have more than one kid, however, you may really need extra space of some kind. Everyone needs to wear clothes, but not everyone needs cargo pants. If you're a contractor, though, a place to keep extra tools is a must.

We've established that Nancy has a lot of things to consider, and these are going to be the variations that make her event different from every event that you've worked with. Many of her guests might be vegetarians, and she wants to make sure they get something really good for dinner, so they don't feel like an afterthought. She may have a children's orchestra performing who need to have a place to warm up their (loud) instruments. Considerations like this have a major effect on how she makes her choice.

In addition to those considerations, what are the variables that are going to swing Nancy toward one solution or another? What else plays into the way she ultimately evaluates her options? Most of the time, price is going to matter, especially to a nonprofit fundraiser like Nancy, who needs to be able to account for every dime. Remember, though, that you don't want to simply sell on price: you want to sell based on value. Knowing how to respond to her considerations above is going to help you bring your company's value to her attention.

You need to think about everything that you've learned about Nancy up until this point as well. You know what failure looks like for her, and you know what stresses her out. Is she going to be able to trust you to be where she needs you to be when she needs you there? Is your equipment going to fail at an important moment, and will you have enough of it to fulfill the baseline need of everyone being able to see and hear? Are you going to be able to give her the right amount of information so she feels that she knows the production side of things is under control and she can go back to wrangling volunteers (or even sit down and enjoy her meal)?

Also, remember that Nancy is part of a nonprofit organization whose mission she loves. At the base of it all, she probably wants to feel comfortable that whoever she works with supports what her organization is doing too.

Step 5: The Customer Makes a Purchase

At last! We've arrived at the end of the sales journey…almost. This is the part most salespeople are comfortable with and the one they often jump to before the customer is ready. But to be fair, there is a reason for that, because it's a critical part of the sales journey. If you don't know how to reduce risk for a customer at this step of the sales journey, it's going to make it almost impossible for them to make the decision to buy.

BUYING PROCESS

How does your target audience persona buy a solution? In this case, you know that this isn't completely up to Nancy alone. As a person who raises funds for a nonprofit, Nancy needs to answer to her board. That means she must have an abundantly clear understanding of the budget and be able to advocate for your company almost as much as you can advocate for yourselves. Be ready to talk with her about payment plans, billing, and even potential discounts sooner rather than later.

CONFIDENCE AND RISK

What can you give Nancy to make her more confident in going with you as her solution? Do you have any references that you can direct her to, who will let you know how well you handled their event? Does she need examples of similar events that you've worked on in the past? Describe any actions she may want you to take or any resources you might be able to give her as she moves toward buying. Let her know whether you have any warranties or guarantees.

FINAL STEP

What is the final action the buyer needs to take to purchase your offer? If you have a contract you need to have Nancy sign in order to get going on the project, make sure she has it when she needs it (probably before she speaks to her board). Let her know how the project will be set in motion and what you need to do to get going on it.

How Do They Fit?

There's incredible value to knowing where a customer is on their sales journey, and there's also value in knowing that the journey isn't linear. Not knowing about the range of emotional space that a customer might inhabit may also threaten your ability to take that last step for them to close.

You may remember that Online Academy has two salespeople who operate in very different ways. Lori is focused on concrete solutions and providing resources to people who are evaluating and considering—usually most comfortable working in steps 4 and 5. The other salesperson in this scenario, Maria, is more comfortable with people who are just beginning their sales journey and takes more of a life-coaching style approach to sales—focusing on steps 1, 2, and 3.

While I was working in a sales coaching capacity at Online Academy, I was able to observe what a major difference it made when salespeople did (or didn't) meet a customer where they were on their sales journey. One day, the director of client services at Online Academy provided a referral to the sales team. It was a friend she thought would be perfect to take one of the courses, so she sent her friend to talk to Maria who, by the numbers, was the most successful and seemed most likely to close the deal.

The next day, the director of client services reached out to me because she knew I worked as a coach with the sales team. "You need to talk with Maria," she said. "My friend didn't like speaking with her at all and decided that our programs weren't a good fit. I know that what we provide would be amazing for her, but she felt like she wasn't getting her questions answered. So, she just got frustrated and isn't interested anymore."

I asked if there was anything in particular that she complained about. "She says Maria kept her on the phone too long talking about *why* she wanted to do the course rather than just giving her the information she needed to evaluate whether the course was a good choice for her or not."

The next week, Maria called me with a similar concern. "You need to talk to Lori. I had a person call who said that they talked with her, but even though they were interested in the course, Lori said they weren't a good fit."

The caller had just begun her sales journey and was thinking about her desired state and how Online Academy's courses might help her, but she wasn't ready to learn the practical details yet. Lori had skipped talking about the caller's current state, challenges, and desired state and went right to solutions. The caller tried again, scheduling another call with Maria this time. Maria met her back at step 1, talking about where she was currently and how the courses could help her with her challenges. After about an hour and a half, the caller enthusiastically purchased a course.

Neither Maria nor Lori were necessarily being poor salespeople. They had just misidentified where their customers were on their sales journeys. If the director of client services' friend had spoken with Lori, who was more interested in step 4 solutions, instead of Maria, who tends to start back at step 1, they may have gotten the information they needed succinctly and decided to buy.

You can see from this story how much it matters for a salesperson to be able to tell where a potential buyer is on their sales journey. That's why it's important to review Sales Foundations and the 5-Step Sales Journey in your weekly sales team meetings. In a chapter 9, I show you how to help your Improvement Team evaluate their own leads and develop a sharper nose for which of the five steps a potential buyer is experiencing.

Building Out the Blueprints

At this point, you may have at least one person on the sales team looking at this 5-Step Sales Journey and thinking, *Well, duh. That's what I do naturally when I sell.*

If that's true, fantastic! That's only the beginning. We're setting the stage here for something bigger than just a salesperson working one-on-one with a customer. Knowing your target audience persona's sales journey adds plans to your Sales Foundations, and these plans are meant to be collaborated upon by the entire Improvement Team. Yes, each salesperson should be able to intuitively sense and meet each person at any point in their journey, but marketing also will build content based on this blueprint, to codify the words that sales use, to bolt this content securely to the Sales Foundations.

Once you have this solid knowledge of your company's value, and now these blueprints to truly know your customer, it's time for sales and marketing to pull on their cargo pants and get to work building Sales Infrastructure.

Chapter 7:
How Will You Sell It?

Organizing Your Sales Infrastructure

If you've ever grown tomatoes, you know what it's like to wait. After staring at a vine covered in green fruit for weeks, it can be tempting to snatch the first one that starts to redden. But if there's still a little bit of green on there and you bite into it, you're going to get a mouth full of stiff, bitter pulp. And then you have one less tomato that could have turned into something delicious.

It was 5:30 p.m. on a Friday, and I had just sat down to play a game with my son when a notification lit up my phone. It was a panicked message from Dave from Online Academy.

We need more revenue. We need to do a 30% off sale to bring in $50K fast, or we're not going to make payroll.

As you might remember from chapter 1, Dave's company had been growing pretty rapidly but also had been resorting to deep discounts in order to survive uncertain times for a while. We had been working hard to get rid of the need for that, though, and I managed to talk him down enough that he agreed to talk Monday instead of right at that moment. I knew from the work we'd done so far that the sales funnel had made some major improvements and had strengthened.

On Monday, I presented him with the data. I showed him how many upcoming appointments there were and the percentage that we expected to close by the end of the month. I also showed him the strength of the current sales pipeline, which included forecasted revenue from leads that had already had at least one appointment with the sales team and had clear next steps to move them toward a purchase. Showing him those numbers, I was able to allay his fears. By the end of the week, we had surpassed that $50,000 mark with what we already had (and without any discounting!).

Continuously running these sales while in a state of high stress would have undermined the natural sales cycle that we'd been working so hard to strengthen. Instead of letting nature take its course, he was itching to pluck underripe tomatoes from the vine. If I hadn't had the KPIs that demonstrated how much money we could forecast right at my fingertips, we would have probably sold the same number of products but made 30 percent less. Then that would have just contributed to the same problem in the following month.

Does this sound like you? Do you feel like you're in survival mode, forced to discount to bring in more revenue month after month, just to meet your expenses?

Now that you know your Sales Foundations and Design, it's time to tighten up your funnel to keep as much revenue inside as possible. With the right processes and the right information, you can be confident that you're sustaining the revenue you need and more.

Making Your Equation Count

When I created the Revenue Equation, I was like most other Decision Makers, believing that leads were the most important things to keep sales growing. I thought most companies would already have the three elements of it in place: their Sales Foundations firmly set, their customer personas and Sales Design known inside and out, and their Sales Infrastructure in place to sell as efficiently as possible.

Spoiler alert—they didn't. So, I created the Revenue Equation to fill that gap.

In a lot of cases, the salespeople are the canaries in the coal mine. If they aren't certain of what they are selling and to whom, leads stop cold after they enter the sales funnel. Without Sales Foundations, Sales Design, and Sales Infrastructure in place, leads balloon at the top of the funnel and create internal stress and frustration when not enough of them convert to revenue, and the others seem to die on the vine. Were they just bad leads, or did the sales and marketing teams not know how to handle them efficiently?

While having your Sales Foundations and Design figured out can do a lot to help motivate salespeople, infrastructure is critical to their being able to do their jobs without stumbling over cracks in the organization. You want your Improvement Team stable, and for them to get there, your sales processes need to run seamlessly.

This chapter is the third factor in your Revenue Equation, and it carefully builds on the last two. This is where you map the work of the Improvement Team directly to the sales journey described in chapter 6. It's a process of organizing all your resources and all your plans so that you can get into action. I show you the three most important parts of establishing your Sales Infrastructure:

- **Organize your resources** so that they are easily available, current, visible, shared, and used consistently and uniformly by the sales and marketing team.
- **Define your funnel** and show how each step of your sales process aligns to different steps of the sales journey, clarifying who owns every step and what actions those owners should take to move the customer from one phase to the next.
- **Manage your team's performance** by developing and measuring goals and KPIs that align with the steps of your sales process; do so by documenting the infrastructure of the sales funnel and its owners to align with marketing and sales technologies and running meetings that are a valuable use of everyone's time.

Once you've spent time planning and living out these steps, you'll be able to stabilize your revenue. Then you can finally start thinking about moving from stabilization to intentional and predictable revenue growth, bringing in more leads and creating more opportunities.

Organize Your Resources

Does this sound familiar to you?

Lori pops into the company Slack channel and says, "Hey, I'm going to be giving a sales presentation webinar in a couple of weeks. Does anyone have the link to that presentation we did a couple of months ago so I can work off it?"

For hours there is no answer, until Jasmine from marketing attaches a PowerPoint presentation with the file name Presentation.final.ppt and says, "I found a copy of it."

Lori starts working from that file, but then Maria attaches a file of her own called Presentation1.final-final.ppt. "I think this is actually the most recent version," she says.

A couple minutes later, Lori messages the group, "These both have the old pricing from before we updated the offerings in December. Can anyone confirm the current pricing for…"

You get the idea.

There are several problems with the way that most people deal with their process for updating, managing, and controlling the versions of their documents and resources at an organizational or team level. Firstly, they are usually managed in a reactive rather than a proactive way. People don't know where something is until someone needs it, so they waste a lot of valuable time digging around for it. Next, there are problems with version control—there are probably multiple copies of something, and without a central location and a comprehensible way of naming and versioning files, it's nearly impossible to figure out what's the most current resource.

Probably worst of all is that once you've gone through working out your Revenue Equation, many of the documents you once used will have out-of-date information. A new marketing manager coming into the organization might find Brandbook.Final.PDF in the file-share and craft an entire landing page around the outdated information inside. Whenever someone else gets around to discovering the error, you might have a lot of work to undo. You may even have lost out on attracting ideal customers.

Creating a Sharing Culture

You should organize your assets to save yourself time and trouble, but when you do, you're also achieving a larger goal of moving toward that vision of a high-performing sales organization.

It's also going to require your sales and marketing team to pool their resources into one spot. Most organizations have their sales and marketing resources siloed, which means that your messaging runs a huge risk of being mismatched. Later in this chapter, I discuss a specific stage in the sales funnel that makes it imperative you bring everything under one roof.

As you commit and recommit to change, you will also be repeating yourself often, and that's okay—in fact, it's encouraged. You may have a file-share or database full of resources, but does your team know where they are? Jasmine may have reminded everyone where the new sales deck was at the last sales and marketing meeting, but if none of the sales team have been able to find it, they'll need to be reminded, even if that means you have to do it at every sales meeting. This is how you create habits, and eventually it will be a regular instinct for your employees to seek resources from a single place.

Not sure how to start putting your most important assets together? Try the following:

- Think about what would happen if a brand-new salesperson started work today. Put yourself in their shoes and think of what resources they might ask for first to do their job.
- Ask the person in charge of each step in the sales funnel what

documents they're tired of people asking them for.

- Think about the resources that, if they were missing, could ruin your chances of making a sale.
- Think about whether you have the documents you need to meet potential customers where they are at each step in the sales journey. Not sure what those documents are or who owns them? Time to figure it out.

The Sales Placemat:

Roles & Responsibilities
Sales Process
KPIs & Performance Management

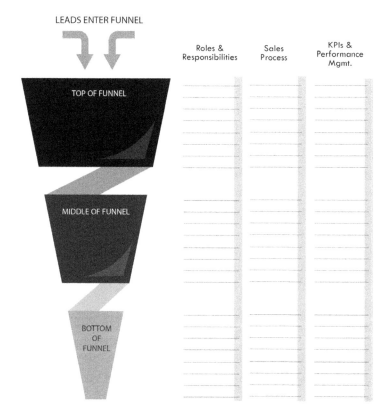

Everyone in Their Right Place

In that diagram, which I like to call the placemat, you can see a simple rendering of a sales funnel. It's designed to help the team understand how to work together to efficiently move customers from the top to the bottom. I often print this out on an eleven-by-seventeen piece of paper and pass it around to clients, asking them to fill it out for me. They often look at me blankly. Maybe they can put "Marketing" at the top of the funnel and "Sales" at the bottom. Often, that's all they can do.

The diagram is a simple way to clarify three things:

- **Roles and Responsibilities:** Who owns each step in the funnel that helps to move a lead to the next stage, and what are their primary responsibilities?
- **Sales Process:** What activities need to take place at each stage of the funnel, according to the sales journey that the potential customer is experiencing? These are the actions we have determined to move the lead from one stage of the sales funnel to the next.
- **Performance Management:** How do we observe and measure that activity, both qualitatively and quantitatively, so that at a later point in time, we can evaluate how successful we are at moving or migrating a lead from one stage to the next?

Can you fill out this diagram for your organization? Can your Improvement Team? If you were a high-performing sales organization, you could. You would be able to do it on a general level, but you would also be able to do it for each of the personas you compiled in your Sales Design process, and ultimately, you would be able to do it for each of your sales and marketing campaigns as well.

If you can't do it right now, though, I have good news. This tool will diagnose exactly where your sales process is breaking down. If you're able to simply map out what fits into each of these columns in the majority of your sales campaigns, you'll be 80 percent of the way to where you want to be. To do that, however, you first need to map your funnel to your customer's sales journey.

Keep in mind, any customer can enter the funnel at any point in the journey. They could find your business with the intent to buy as soon as possible and enter at the bottom of the funnel. They might not even know they need what you are offering yet and enter at the top because they were curious to learn more about you from a magnet or social media post they came across. For the purposes of this map, you are going to imagine that your ideal customer is moving linearly through each stage of the funnel. Knowing what you need to do and who needs to do it allows you to be more efficient and create a frictionless journey that can get more streamlined over time.

Then we start to assign measurements, KPIs, which become the numeric representations of how effective the strategies are to move that person from one stage to the next. By doing this, you complete a journey without any breaks in it to guide that sales lead from the top of the funnel to the bottom.

Sales Funnel Stage 1—The Top of the Funnel
Characteristic: "I Want to Learn."

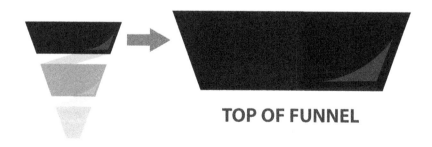

TOP OF FUNNEL

The top of the funnel is often associated with MQLs, or Marketing Qualified Leads.

This stage of the funnel tends to map with steps 1–3 of the 5-Step Sales Journey discussed in chapter 6: the customer's current state, challenges, and desired state. This is the point where your typical prospect, who should be one of your target audience personas, enters the funnel. Your potential customer is just starting to look for solutions to their problems. They are not ready to buy. You are aiming to pique their interest and start educating them. Here, you meet your customer in their current state and offer them education that will draw them in to learn more and move toward their desired state.

ROLES AND RESPONSIBILITIES

This stage typically belongs to marketing. At some organizations, the role could fall to one person, while at others it might be three or more. The typical owners of this stage are in the leadership roles of marketing: CMO, VP of marketing, marketing director, or marketing manager. Their responsibilities are to educate and prime leads in this stage so that they get more interested in the company and the company's solutions, ultimately preparing the leads for the next stage of the funnel. Remember that when you fill out this phase on your placemat, you should be naming each individual who is involved in planning, producing, and tracking of all of these stages.

SALES PROCESS

For Nonprofit Nancy, one of our United Events' ideal target personas, the actions we'd take at this stage would be focused on providing highly relevant content that strengthens her connection with United Events, supports her in her job, and primes her to want to learn more about United Events and their solutions. Ultimately, we are looking for the actions in this stage to keep United Events at the top of Nancy's mind and build a bridge that Nancy wants to travel across to talk with the sales team.

These actions could include marketing automation emails that provide a series of resources over a period of three to four weeks with automation triggers that send additional information based on how the lead interacts with the emails. It could be invitations to private Facebook channels or webinars or on-demand videos or an invitation to connect on LinkedIn. This group will typically also begin to receive your newsletters.

PERFORMANCE MANAGEMENT

At the top of the funnel, we're looking for data that can provide us with information about acquisition sources and populations, lead actions or activities, and give you the ability to segment or organize.

Gather information about where your populations are coming from, the total population in the stage, whether the population is increasing or decreasing, and the conversion rates and conversion timing from this stage to the next. This includes open rates on the emails we send these leads, as well as click-through rates for calls to action.

You want to segment populations according to their behavior, such as whether they respond to calls to action to do further reading or register for webinars. You'll be analyzing the data later on to figure out which resources are most valuable to your audience. By recording and reviewing this data, you can analyze the effectiveness of these actions, create performance baselines, and test improvements to see if they create increases in performance.

Sales Funnel Stage 2—The Middle of the Funnel
Characteristic: "I Want More."

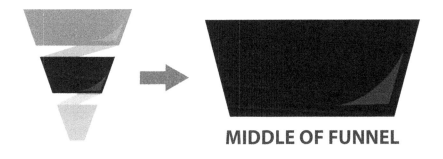

MIDDLE OF FUNNEL

The middle of the funnel is often associated with SQLs, or Sales Qualified Leads.

This stage of the funnel is often a combination of steps 3 and 4 (desired state and solutions), where people move from their current state to considering solutions. Some of those solutions may be yours. At this point, the resources you offer can move from educating your customer on ways to solve their problem generally ("How to Evaluate Outside Event Vendors") to offering your own services as that solution ("The United Events Approach to an Effective Fundraiser"). By now, you have provided your customers with enough education on the different solutions available to them that they are ready to hear your case for why you might be their best choice. In fact, they are at the point where they may be starting to envision what their life might be like if they did buy your product.

Consider this example: Let's say I've been thinking about buying a new car. I start by educating myself on buying and choosing a car, looking at features online, looking at consumer reports, and maybe reading reviews and asking around to see what kinds of cars people like me are buying.

Then, a particular car—the Tesla Model 3—catches my eye, and something clicks. I've heard conflicting reviews, but at this point, I am interested enough to start orbiting the Tesla website and social media accounts. I'm not just thinking about "a car" anymore. I have my eye on that brand of car and ultimately a particular model (though I might have my eye on a couple other cars that are in a similar category too).

I am now in stage 2 of the funnel. I'm not just considering general solutions—I am considering a particular solution and trying to envision what my life would look like if I chose to buy. I'm daydreaming about zipping around town in my new Tesla, but that's all it is right now—a daydream.

The trickiest part of the funnel for your sales organization is this stage. This is where your sharing culture is most needed, where marketing and sales must work together and must not be cordoned off from one another. Here, you are most likely to lose track of potential customers who you might successfully sell to if only they had more information and personal contact. If only they had someone who had really shown them that *your* solution was right *for them* specifically.

Above all, this is the stage of the funnel where you want to be intentional about using your Sales Infrastructure.

ROLES AND RESPONSIBILITIES

Sales and marketing work together on this one, in a combined effort of observing customer behavior, tracking KPIs, reaching out with relevant content, and reaching out with targeted and even personal responses.

This stage is where there are a ton of potential sales waiting to be unlocked. But it's a tricky place too because it's that transitional place between marketing and sales. We need marketing to keep priming these leads and identifying the leads that have the best potential for sales to begin to interact with in a one-on-one and personal way. There is a continuum of the sales readiness of these leads, and that's actually where some of the greatest value of this exercise gets unlocked. If you want to increase your intentionality and success, you need to realize there are two types of leads at this stage. One type are leads that, if directly contacted by sales, could be primed to learn more about your solutions and accelerate their journey to becoming customers. And leads that are proactively reaching out to sales themselves.

The people responsible for this stage will be in the sales team with titles like business development representative, sales development representative, salesperson, account executive, and account manager. Their responsibilities are to engage leads that are ready to learn more about the company and offerings. This is about becoming an expert at discovery, building rapport and relationships, and providing the leads with resources and information that enable them to make clear decisions on the value your company provides.

SALES PROCESS

The sales process includes all the activities that need to be done to move a lead through this crucial stage of the funnel, turning leads who are interested in your solutions into leads who want to purchase.

General steps in this phase of the process include:

- More solution-based email sequences
- One-on-one outreach via phone or personal email
- Individualized emails with information based on researching the lead
- Activities or resources that provide additional information on your offerings
- Invitations to webinars, group presentations, or demos
- Product demonstrations or sample runs

Let's return to the Tesla example, and let's say that my curiosity has brought me to the Tesla website, and I have customized my favorite Tesla. Now let's say there is functionality that if I set up an account, I can take my newly spec'd-out Tesla for a virtual test drive. I've done the simulation a couple of times (okay, maybe more than a couple).

I've also provided my phone number on the account and given the dealership permission to contact me. But I'm still daydreaming, and I'm a little shy about taking the step of making a purchase or even visiting a nearby showroom or dealership. After all, it's a pretty big decision to buy a new car.

But the marketing team has been tracking my engagement and has run reports that show the sales team all of the accounts that have taken the virtual test drive more than three times. These leads are arguably sales ready, but just as I might make my way to their dealership or even buy the car sight unseen, I might just as easily keep my potential purchase in the daydream category and let time keep going by.

What if, instead, the sales team reached out and invited me to check out a Tesla with a special offer?

The sales development representative calls me and says, "I noticed you've gone on a couple simulated test drives in our Model 3. What would you say if we had someone pick you up at work to go for a real test drive?"

The bridge from marketing to sales has now been crossed because, yes—I would absolutely say yes to that. I've had my eye on this particular car from this particular dealership, and now I'm in touch with a real salesperson, who I'm about to meet in person and develop a relationship with.

PERFORMANCE MANAGEMENT

As I mentioned earlier, this is the stage that should be a constant subject of measurement, analysis, and discussion among your sales and marketing teams. We'll be talking about the recommended way to hold those conversations later on. Meanwhile, you'll be judging KPIs according to how people in your funnel choose to continue to engage with your content, or not to engage. The data you collect should identify populations and segmentations that may have changed from the top of the funnel as well as acceleration levers, sticking points, deal killers where people either exit or get stuck in the funnel, and the lead's time in stage.

Sales Funnel Stage 3—The Bottom of the Funnel
Characteristic: "I Want to Buy."

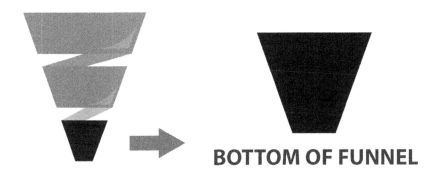

BOTTOM OF FUNNEL

The bottom of the funnel is often associated with opportunities or deals. Congratulations! You made it through the most difficult stage of the funnel, and your prospect is very close to buying. Usually customers in this stage are late in step 4 or already in step 5 of their sales journey. This is the stage where your sales team is likely the most comfortable, especially with all the work you've done with your Sales Foundations and all you know about your target persona. Your team knows what sets you apart and why your company's service is going to fit with the customer's specific needs.

ROLES AND RESPONSIBILITIES
This is the point where sales really shine; however, marketing can offer support through the assets they've already created—case studies, infographics, or other content that customers can use to de-risk their decision.

SALES PROCESS
Be ready with those resources in your asset library. Know the uniform language that's in alignment with the Sales Foundations you and your team have decided on. Have case studies on hand for customers

who are similar to your target persona. And if you're the sales manager, know your salespeople's individual strengths in case backup is needed—like how Maria's style of selling worked with one customer's needs while Lori's didn't. (I talk more about your Improvement Team's strengths in the next chapter.)

PERFORMANCE MANAGEMENT

Here in the bottom of the funnel, tracking the percentage of customers that you close, and how long it takes to close them, is vital for being able to forecast your income. The fact that I had those numbers from this stage was the reason I was able to talk the CEO of Online Academy down from his ledge and keep the company from losing money on sales that were already—almost—in the bag. In chapter 9, I talk about how those numbers can also help you find ways to tighten your funnel, boost revenue, and make long-term forecasts. To be able to make those crucial interpretations that move your revenue to the next level, be sure to track close rates, time in stage or aging opportunities, last actions before purchase, pricing and discounts, payment terms, and nonstandard or custom solutions, deals, or orders.

How to Run Meaningful Meetings

I've repeatedly emphasized the importance of bringing sales and marketing together and committing and recommitting to trust, shared assets, and open communication in order to keep the machine running in top condition.

Think of your weekly sales meetings as tune-ups for that engine. If people miss them, or if they start falling by the wayside, you'll find that the engine will start breaking down more often. Your mileage will suffer, and you'll start leaking revenue.

Most of the sales meetings I've been to have consisted of the person leading saying, "Rick, you go first; tell us what's going on." Then, one by one, you go around the table giving each person an unspecified amount of time to talk about themselves and their accounts. It's often unfocused and almost always unnecessary. Because of this tendency, many, many people dread sales meetings and don't think of them as valuable.

That's not what you'll be doing. Your sales meetings will be one of the most important, if not the most important, part of your Improvement Team's week. Purpose-driven, clear outcomes reinforce the work you have done, and those who attend will leave feeling like they've moved together both as an individual and a group.

Here are a few ground rules.

1. You agree on a time every week, and everyone blocks out that time in their calendar to attend. Nothing will be scheduled during that standing meeting, including sales calls, except if there is a major emergency (like if your house is burning down). Part of this agreement is that everyone there is on time (early is best) and that you always end on time.

2. You stick to fifty to fifty-five minutes, no matter what. Your salespeople should be able to leave the meeting in time to make it to any appointments scheduled at the top of the hour. This honors their time, maintaining trust, and it also models the way that you expect them to respect their customer's time.

3. The team needs to be fully focused. This meeting has tremendous value, and anything that dilutes that value is not okay. Make an agreement that they cannot work on other things while they are in the meeting. However, there could be exceptions. In your own organization, you can create the exceptions that your team can agree with, for example, if a salesperson is waiting on an urgent call or promised something to a lead or customer by a specific time and needs to check their email because they are waiting on a teammate to get the information. If you do make these agreements, let the person know that when this exception happens, it's acceptable for them to leave

the meeting to deal with the pressing business and then come back when they're done.

Now that you have the basics down, here's the agenda I recommend.

Team-Based Business Development: 0–10 Minutes

While you need to be rigid about holding this meeting, you should offer some flexibility for when people come and go. After all, their highest priority is their customers. If they are about to close a sale, they shouldn't feel compelled to immediately jump off the phone so they won't be late to the meeting. These first few minutes give a little bit of buffer time.

Usually I do a couple of things:

- We do a quick check-in with the company's social media feeds, and I encourage every team member to share some of the company's content on their LinkedIn profiles or any other social media platform that is relevant to the company's work.
- We discuss any upcoming events or opportunities to network with potential customers or deepen relationships with current customers, new resources that marketing is rolling out, or up-coming webinars or panel discussions.

Sales Performance: 10–20 Minutes

This is an opportunity for salespeople to learn from one another and get ideas for ways they can solve their own problems. It's also a great way to celebrate, acknowledge, and inspire—all of which builds stronger, higher-performing teams.

- Everyone gets two minutes to share one win from the week and one lesson learned.
- We discuss upcoming sales initiatives or ones that are running currently. This is an area where you'll probably have to repeat yourself.

Just as you have to remind people where to find the vital sales assets, it's worth it to repeat important information. Whatever it takes to get everyone in alignment is priority number one.

- Discuss sales funnel reports—how strong they are and what they'll probably be able to close in the next couple of weeks. This includes leading indicators like the seven-day average of the number of new appointments booked or the number of new leads entering the funnel each day, the number of follow-up calls the team has booked, and where the team is in relation to revenue goals.
- Brainstorm quick wins and ways to easily bring in revenue. Does one of your salespeople have a potential customer who says they'd be more willing to buy if you offered net sixty instead of net thirty? Maybe other people around the circle have potential customers who have said something similar. Just asking your salespeople about what they are seeing and hearing can help you figure out where to direct your focus faster than computer-generated reports.

Working Session: 15–20 Minutes

Some people are so organized that they put an hour or so aside every day to develop tools that will help them do their work. Maybe it's a custom spreadsheet that gives them specific information, a series of CRM reports that track where all their leads are in the sales funnel, or a set of email templates they use when they reach out to leads. These people are rare birds, though. That's why I like to set aside fifteen to twenty minutes in every meeting to provide structured time for them to do something proactive that will move them, and the company, an inch or two forward.

The big winners for working sessions include:

- Email templates the sales team can use for outreach to a specific type of lead (that is at a specific stage of the sales funnel) and the time in the meeting for each salesperson to send five to ten emails

- Review of new reports or CRM functionality that will make the sales team's life better, increase their efficiency, and shorten the sales cycle
- Strategies to improve how the team sells and corresponding role-play to ensure each salesperson understands and can implement them
- Review of any organizational changes that affect how the sales team operates and interacts with other departments
- Discussions about improvements to the sales process or the company's offerings
- Firsthand observations and feedback from marketing campaigns or new product features, a time to gather the feedback from the eyes and ears of the company—the sales team.

Housekeeping and Wrap-Up: 5–10 Minutes

These last ten minutes are disposable, and they can be skipped if you are about to run over your allotted time, or salespeople can leave if they have calls they need to attend. This is where you make announcements that you can later send out over email, or you can address anything that may have been put into the parking lot. You can also identify people on the team who might have something they want to talk with you about one-on-one.

Completing Your Revenue Equation

So, you've made it through the last step in your Revenue Equation. You now have a complete manual for how your sales organization will best operate. Next, we're going to talk about how each individual salesperson can bring their best by aligning their work goals with their life goals. Then, we'll talk about how you can get a hold on all the revenue that, until now, has been trapped inside the funnel waiting to be discovered. Finally, we'll talk about how to develop and prioritize strategies and tactics to get to your revenue goal.

Framework #2:

The Individual Performance Planner

Chapter 8:
The Individual
Performance Planner

Getting Your Sales Team Behind the Wheel

So, you've worked with your team to build out the three factors of your Revenue Equation, complete with a guide that shows you how to keep it stable and leave room for growth. Now the question is, how will your team commit to consistently operating the efficient machine that you've just built?

Welcome to the second framework to stabilizing and growing your business's revenue: the Individual Performance Planner.

Once you've balanced your Revenue Equation, it's time to look around the room at the people who are going to bring it into the real world. You're going to do the same thing you did for the Revenue Equation for each of the people who collaborated to build it in the first place. You are going to have each salesperson create an Individual Performance Planner for themselves to use as a manual to their own performance (and happiness).

You might think that they should be able to do this on their own without input—to manage themselves and make sure they're following the rules that everyone has set up together. In almost every way, they will be doing this themselves, but not *alone*. Using this template doesn't make your salespeople into little robots, creating a rote process. If every customer moves through the sales journey differently, so will every salesperson. This just helps them put together a road map to get that done in a way that fits their strengths.

The Individual Performance Planner covers:

- Who your salesperson is and what their strengths are
- What they want, both inside and outside of work
- Who their biggest customers are
- How they can use their strengths to reach those customers
- What would best support their ability to improve and reach revenue goals
- The performance—and personal—goals that they have committed to

And it should especially matter to sales managers because this manual, though at its core for the salesperson, will help managers manage a team that is doing their absolute best. It's like having an instruction manual for every salesperson you lead. It shows you exactly what they value, what motivates them, and how you can best support them. It also helps the salesperson to clearly articulate who they are and what they need from the sales manager and company for them to be the best they can be.

You win, they win, and the company wins.

Why Do an Individual Performance Planner?

When I first come into an organization and talk with the Decision Makers, I usually talk to them about their salespeople. What are they like? How are they performing? Who are their customers? What are their trouble spots?

There are as many types of salespeople as there are stars in the sky, each bringing their own personalities and problems. Rick from United Events, for example, was great at building and maintaining relationships but was overly cautious about finding new prospects because he hated to be rejected. Some salespeople are better on their own, and others prefer the validation and input that comes with working as a team. Some are self-starters, and some need external motivation. Some are determined to get down to business, like Lori from the Online Academy, while others prefer to have longer, more abstract discussions, like Maria.

In every group, there's usually one "lone wolf" salesperson, who is a top performer and may outsell many of the other salespeople and also (as you might have guessed from the nickname) hates doing things like attending meetings and logging customer details in the CRM. Regardless of that salesperson's lack of cooperation, Decision Makers in a company that is struggling with sales tend to be hyper-focused on that result. To them, the ability of that single salesperson to bring in revenue is paramount.

"If I could have all my employees be just like this one," they'll say to me when we first start working together, "then all my problems will be solved."

As we've learned by now, there is no one thing that will solve all your problems, and by definition, you can't create a sales team full of lone wolves. You've just done all this work to create a consensus about who you are as a company, who your customers are and how to communicate with them, and what the best processes and protocols are to keep the sales organization running. Hopefully by now you will have observed how much this Revenue Equation depends on the work of multiple people. Instead of relying on a lone wolf to hunt down and close new customers, you have just created a purpose-built plan to deal with leads at each stage of their sales journey. This means you'll not only attract the leads but maintain and eventually multiply them. You want a team who continues to hold that vision and work toward it together.

The prospect of people acting outside of their expectations, and often the fear of people leaving, can do a psychological number on leaders. That's perfectly normal.

You might be thinking, *Do I really want my salespeople to do this? What if they fill this Individual Performance Planner out and I realize I don't want them at this company? What if they fill this out and they realize that* they *don't want to be at this company?* It's especially stressful to think about this type of shake-up for small and family businesses. Maybe one of the salespeople is a friend of your cousins, and whether they work for your company or not, you're going to have to see them at next year's Fourth of July barbeque. Talk about awkward!

This may be hard to hear, but you have to be okay with that, because ultimately, people do have free choice. It's true that by this point, lone wolf salespeople who aren't willing to run with the pack will probably decide to move on, just like the person who thought that their Ritz-Carltonesque business was more like Costco. Someone might start working on their planner and decide that they don't like selling and would rather go get their SCUBA license. If you truly want change in your organization, and you truly want a high-performing sales organization, then you want a sales team who really wants to be there.

Fortunately, I have not had the experience where this step hasn't created a better reality for individuals on the team. To date, even though that possibility still exists, I've never seen a salesperson who fills out the Individual Performance Planner and then says, "You know what? I'm out of here."

There's more good news: you as a Decision Maker at your company can create the environment that will make people want to stay and keep doing their best. Creating and regularly reviewing and updating the Individual Performance Planner is a big way to do that.

Why Do It Now?

So, why wait until after you've completed the work establishing your Sales Foundation, Design, and Infrastructure? Creating this plan upfront might feel like the natural way to improve your sales, to set individual goals for each of the salespeople, but it could end up causing the kind of problems we've just talked about—people will be tying themselves into knots trying to fit what they think is your vision rather than doing things in the way that they, personally, do best.

You might also be thinking, *I don't have time to bend over backward to coax people into doing work that they should be doing anyway.* I counter that by saying you'll spend more time bending over backward trying to stay organized and scraping up revenue if you don't go through this process than if you do.

By the time United Events brought me in to help prepare them to bring in a new director of sales, they had gone through three directors already; those had each only lasted about a year. One of the owners had been serving in that position, but he didn't want to do it, and he didn't really know how. They needed someone to come in who would stay and help fix some of the problems that they needed solved.

However, when they sent me that list of problems, it was much the same as what I'd seen from other companies I'd worked with—a page full of systemic misalignments and ideas for the "one thing" that could make everything better.

For example, they had some major concerns that their salespeople just weren't selling enough. In addition to having lower sales numbers than was ideal, the team was also a reactive bunch who always seemed to be unhappy and on edge. I knew that true sales ability is often cloaked by ineffective leadership and a lack of clarity for the salespeople. I was confident that addressing those problems would lift the burden of some of those cultural problems. I told them that what they needed to do to sustain and then grow was deal with these root problems by going through each of the steps in the Revenue Equation.

"Let's fix these foundations first, and then we'll strengthen each of your salespeople and bring them together as a team," I said. "Once we do that, it will be a hell of a lot easier for you to bring in a director of sales." When I was done with them, hopefully, that new sales manager wouldn't feel like a coach brought in to sweep the finals, only to discover the players haven't been practicing. They agreed to let me help get the sales team into top form.

I make it a rule to always believe in the team and the individual salespeople, and I believe in making them the best they can be. The happier and more successful they are, the more we let them play to their strengths, the happier they'll be in their everyday lives, and the better they're going to perform at the company. So far, that belief has only produced positive results for everyone.

"So, when we do bring in the new director of sales," I said, "they will have a blueprint of what's important to your employees and know how best to work with them. Wouldn't you like your next manager to look at your salesperson and say, 'I get this person pretty well, and now I have a tool to help me learn what they need from me. I know how to meet them where they are.' Wouldn't you like that?"

Wouldn't you?

That's why we're doing this. That's why it's worth the additional time and energy to create these planners once you have balanced your Revenue Equation.

Introducing the Individual Performance Planner to Your Team

Put yourself in your salespeople's shoes, whether you are the Change Agent, the Champion, a Decision Maker, or whoever is leading the sales team. If someone you'd only recently met handed you several pages of questions asking about your strengths, needs, preferences, and top customers, you'd probably feel kind of uneasy about it. Depending on what the company culture has been up until now, you might even be suspicious. Are you going to be judged, even fired, for your answers? Are you going to be able to answer truthfully, or is there some expected response that you're going to have to guess at?

Going back to United Events, I had a challenge with the sales team going in. I'd already been made aware that there were tensions, distrust, and even some reactive behavior on the team. I couldn't just jump in and start asking them personal questions.

Because I started by asking questions about the company, I was able to get them to engage without them having to reveal a lot of information about themselves from the start. I created a container—a place where I, as the Change Agent, could cultivate and nurture growth. Through this process, they could see how their input was valued, and through the process of cocreating this vision, they started to feel a greater sense of ownership in the company.

Often this process naturally leads to self-exploration. If you're talking together about how to represent the company's values and understand the ideal customer's journey and about who owns what for each step, they're already thinking about their current contributions and how they might adjust. When it comes time to work on the Individual Performance Planner, they are able to make the connection.

We did it for the company—now we're doing it for ourselves.

Completing the Individual Performance Planner

Let's dive into what each salesperson will be writing as they create their personal blueprint for how to conduct business every day to reach their larger sales goals. I'm going to use Jackie, the high-performing salesperson from United Events, as an example and describe how I as Change Agent encouraged her, in one-on-ones and in collaborative discussion with the rest of the group.

On its face, we were making a plan for Jackie to sell better, but we were also planning how she, as an individual, could be clearer about what she wanted. That means she examined a lot more than what happened between the time she sat down at her desk and when she walked out the door for the day. She is a whole person, not just a salesperson—she's also a mom, a daughter, a community leader, and probably a lot of other things that her manager has no idea about.

Whether you are Jackie's manager or the Change Agent helping her complete this Planner, you have to coach and encourage the whole human being, not just this one piece of who she is. This may be a plan for better sales, but that first word, "individual," is what matters most.

Strengths and Focus Areas

This section gives insights into the salesperson's personal strengths and your daily focus areas. It asks the participants to answer the following questions.

- What are your strengths?
- How could you use more of your strengths each day?
- What is your focus most days?
- What is your ideal focus each day?
- What might enable you to spend more time on your ideal focus areas?

IDENTIFYING AND USING YOUR STRENGTHS

When I asked Jackie about her strengths, she wrote that she was goal oriented. From this information alone, I could adjust my approach as a manager.

"Oh, you're goal oriented. Okay. Do you want me to help you create a goal and help you keep moving toward it?" If that was truly one of her strengths, this would be an effective way to help her improve her performance. Now Jackie felt understood, and as her Change Agent, I knew how to help her.

When you are managing a sales team, you probably see sets of overlapping skills at first. As you see them continue to investigate, you find plenty of differences that help you know where each of them needs to be deployed.

Then we discuss how they can use their strengths daily. In some cases, they may feel that they already use their strengths daily. However, if a salesperson doesn't see things that way, they give me as their manager a way to improve their day. By creating awareness for them, they can start to advocate for themselves. And that's what this is all about—their ability to advocate for themselves and make sure the manager wants to help them be the person they're declaring, through this planner, that they want to be.

IDENTIFYING AND USING OPTIMAL FOCUS AREAS

When referring to the salesperson's focus, it's all about awareness of their current state and projecting ways that they can reach their ideal state. So, where are they focusing most days, and what would they like to be focusing on instead? Both manager and salesperson can start thinking of ways the company can put them to their highest and best use every day. Maybe there are obstacles to this that a manager might be able to remove. There are two lenses of self-awareness here: one for the salesperson to see their way to self-advocating and one for the manager to uncover the resources this person needs to operate their best.

TEAM AND THE INDIVIDUAL PLANNER

As with all the discussions that the Change Agent has led until now, this one needs to be organized in a way that maintains trust and leads toward a clear objective. It also needs to take into account the team's comfort sharing their individual answers with one another and whether that's a productive use of time and energy.

When I have facilitated this, I start with each person working through the planner themselves, then hold a one-on-one meeting, and then—if the team is small enough—I bring them all together. If your sales team is comfortable enough with each other, I'd recommend this, but that requires the Change Agent be very aware of their states. If it's a closer team, you can do a longer exercise. While the Individual Performance Planner is a personal tool, having the input of the team can really help salespeople come to see their own potential. The benefit is collaboration, a better sense of community, and the mutual respect to be more generous with time.

Let's go back to Jackie. I brought the other salespeople into the room and asked her if she was comfortable sharing three of the top strengths she put into her planner. To make her more comfortable, I did a couple of things: I didn't put her list on the screen we were all viewing as a group. Then, once she was done, rather than opening the discussion for the whole team's input, I selected one teammate to respond.

"Tyrone, is there anything that stood out to you or something that you think she missed?"

"I think it's true that you're creative," Tyrone said, "but I also think you're an excellent communicator, and I didn't hear that on your list."

Tyrone pointing out a new strength came as a surprise to Jackie; it was something she'd never seen in herself. She could add that to a planner and keep it in mind as a problem-solving tool moving forward.

If you don't feel comfortable on the team, or there's too big of a team, or you already have too much team politics, don't do it. If you're at a place where you can ask your team and you're pretty sure they're going to say yes, then a team setting is a great opportunity for growth.

Either way, a one-on-one meeting between a salesperson and manager is a must; take them out to lunch, do it over coffee. Just do it in a way where you turn off your tech and it's all about that individual.

Motivations and Motivators

What drives your team day in and day out? Determining why they even come into work in the morning is vital, and this determination needs to be made in a nonjudgmental way. You don't need to enforce a "correct" motivation for your salespeople, but you need to seek to understand the deepest root of it. To be able to do that, you'll be asking them the following questions.

- How do you describe motivators?
- What motivates you personally? Professionally?
- How do you feel when you achieve or experience your motivations?
- What do you wish you could do more of that would fill you up?

- What ideas do you have that would allow you to achieve more of what fills you up?

PROFESSIONAL MOTIVATORS

United Events initially hired me because of their need for a director of sales, and the time had finally come for me to interview candidates. When I was leading the final interview, I decided to make it both an interview and a live coaching session. The way this person was coachable and interacted with me, in addition to their skills, was super important, and it was something that I was excited about.

"We're pretty sure we want to hire you," I said to him, "so let's get into action and see if this is going to work."

He was excited about this new type of interview and coaching hybrid I'd introduced, based on hypothetical scenarios. One of the questions I asked him was what motivated him at his very core.

Confidently he said, "Money." It wasn't an unusual answer for someone in sales, so I dug deeper to ask what it was about the money that motivated him.

"I want to get rewarded for all my knowledge and hard work, and money is the way that I see that happening."

"So, are you motivated by money or acknowledgment for hard work?" I asked. "And for all your experience?"

He took a moment and then answered more thoughtfully. "Karl, I've done this a long time, and maybe it's my ego talking, but it's really important for me to feel like I'm really good at this, that people know that, and that my reputation grows so that I'm somebody people turn to because of how good I am."

He didn't say money this time, but to him, money was the material thing that represented that deep, internal motivation. What he really wanted were opportunities for recognition and to show the target audience, our industry, that he really knew what he was doing (though money, of course, was still a major factor).

"That's exactly what I need," he said when I repeated my understanding back to him.

I went on. "Would you want part of your job to be going to events where you're speaking on behalf of the company? Say, once or twice a quarter you go out and speak to an audience. And what if we tie compensation to the number of events you went and spoke at?"

We'd nailed it. In our hybrid interview and coaching session, we'd drilled to the core of what truly powered him. Now the person managing him would be able to design ways to align what they needed with what he needed to keep him moving. And after we hired him, that would be codified as a resource to check in on periodically.

PERSONAL MOTIVATORS

As discussed earlier, it's not only professional and sales goals that must be accounted for when individual planning is at play. Jackie, for example, was motivated by both a professional and a personal need to stay balanced, healthy, and seeing the fruits of her efforts.

To Jackie, money was important too, but it was not only that. While she wanted to be appreciated for what she brought to her job every day, money was less a measure of her professional worth than a tool for her to live a happy life.

I knew that she was interested in remodeling her back deck because she wanted more room for her kids to play and for entertaining guests, so when she said, "I want to work from home two days a week," I also knew why.

When I looked at her list of motivators, I saw, "Being appreciated—not being treated like a cog."

"What does being appreciated mean to you, Jackie?" I said, "Is it more money?"

"No, I just want to be trusted enough that I'm allowed to work from home. When I have to come in, that's two hours I lose that I could have spent with my family. Plus, if I get to stay home on a weekday, I can have contractors come in and work while I'm there."

Knowing this about Jackie, I was then able to help her organize a plan to be able to make that happen. Often, salespeople hold wishes like this inside of them because they don't know how to bring it up. To them, it doesn't seem like a possibility if all their manager cares about is their sales records, not the fact that they are human beings with lives outside of the office.

Having a happier sales team, I've found, usually results in better performance. That can only happen when you examine the true roots of their motivations.

Personal and Professional Goals

I start with asking the salespeople to complete two lists: one for their ninety-day and twelve-month goals for their personal lives and another for their professional lives. Then, we list their top three goals for the next three to five years, both personal and professional, and list anything that might get in the way of them achieving those.

It might not be immediately clear to you what personal goals have to do with your company or how your day-to-day operations make a difference. There are a million invisible influences that you might not notice. I find that when people talk about their goals out loud, they become much more real to both the individual and the manager. You might have a better time understanding how those invisible influences could stand in the way of your salesperson's goals, and as a result negatively impact their happiness and success at work.

Jackie put in her list of twelve-month personal goals, "Become healthier and more active."

When I asked whether there was something at the company that was preventing her from being healthier, she first said, "Well, when you book meetings and we order in, there aren't any vegetarian options for me. You're bringing in barbeque, and all I can eat are the beans and cornbread."

It was a simple change, but it was something that was clearly on her mind and influenced her enjoyment of work. Little things that we as a company could easily adjust would greatly ease her anxiety and make it so much easier for her to reach her goals.

If she hadn't had this opportunity to bring it up, I never would have known. It was another big aha moment. If you do this with your salespeople, you'll undoubtedly experience a lot of moments like these. If you have the flexibility to adjust your policies to the needs of your people, it's probably not going to cost you much extra than if you guessed at what they might like. To them, however, it can make a major difference in their level of happiness and meeting their goals without running into these barriers.

Daily Activities and Priorities

This section evaluates each salesperson's highest and best use of their time. It asks the salesperson to:

- Write a list of the things they find themselves doing on a daily or near daily basis
- Select which of those daily activities are low value or have low relevance to their jobs
- Determine which are distractions from their job
- List how many of the meetings they attend each week that are high value and aligned to their highest and best-use activities, versus low value and not aligned
- Consider how they can change their week to optimize their job performance and better achieve their personal and professional goals

Daily prioritization switches gears from the past three topics, and the Change Agent should be aware that it might be a scary question for people to answer. After all, if they're doing these tasks daily, they might feel like disavowing those duties is going to reflect badly on them. If they're reluctant to write them down for their manager to see, or to admit them in a group meeting, have them bring those tasks to your one-on-one. You'll have built up enough trust by now that they should be comfortable discussing these with you.

In our one-on-one, Jackie said, "Meetings that drag on are the biggest time suck for me."

"How so?"

"In almost every sales meeting, they say it's going to be forty-five minutes, but then it goes over an extra twenty. I lose a whole hour I could be using for customer calls because I can't schedule something at 12:20."

It's clear in this example how such a discussion can benefit the company. If she didn't have to waste extra time in these meetings, she'd be able to schedule calls and have more contact time with customers. (By the way, this meeting complaint is incredibly common in most organizations. If you have a problem with inefficient meetings, be sure to review the instructions in the previous chapter for the schedule I use to keep sales meetings efficient.)

Other types of time sinks can include time spent wading through email threads that don't concern them or even dealing with certain customers. Using and reviewing this planner can give managers insight into which salespeople get value out of certain types of meetings and which of them don't. For example, some of your salespeople might not need as much help with the CRM and could focus on something different during a working session.

Managers can also help them discover ways they can offer support and save each other time in customer relations, but we'll get into that a little later.

Community Involvement, Networking, and Education

Salespeople are asked to look at their schedules and ask themselves where they want to be more involved, where they want to grow community and spend time outside of work. Each salesperson lists the following:

- Organizations or associations they would want to be involved in and their desired level of involvement
- Networking groups or networking opportunities they would want to be involved in and their desired level of involvement
- Educational opportunities or skills they would want to learn
- How the organization could support them to achieve this involvement

Learning and community involvement provide an organic way for salespeople to meet new people or beef up the types of activities that help them be more effective. This ended up being the key for Rick to discover an inroad to more high-value customers, when he joined the board of a local nonprofit and was introduced to many people just like United Events' customer persona Nonprofit Nancy.

Tyrone decided to dive in to learning more about the audiovisual process and spent time outside of work assisting with sound production for local musical performances. While it didn't exactly make him want to get into the production side of the company, these activities gave him the confidence to discuss with potential customers how their equipment could enhance events.

As a manager, if you see your salespeople all wanting to learn about the same thing—public speaking, for example—it gives you an opportunity to arrange for workshops and team-oriented activities that build everyone's skills and their relationships with one another.

Sales Targets, Current Customers, and Measuring Success

Jackie had most of her planner completed. It was about her strengths, what motivated her, what her personal goals were, how she prioritized her day, the involvement she wanted in the community, and the additional education she wanted. We then let Jackie self-determine the sales targets she felt like she could get. The latter half of the Individual Performance Planner ignites the fuel of the first half and spurs the salespeople to action.

First, team members create sales targets for the next ninety days and the next twelve months, along with their plans to reach those goals. Having them self-select their goals makes a major difference versus it coming from the top down.

If I said to Jackie, "In the next ninety days, I need you to do A, B, C, and D," with no knowledge of who she is, what she's dealing with in her life, or what obstacles she's facing, she would most likely leave angry. But if she got to determine her own sales targets for the next ninety days, especially when she understood she had her manager's support, there would be a really good chance she'd aim as high as she could.

Now you ask the salesperson to identify the top five leads in their funnel and how they think they need to move them toward closing.

- Who are they?
- What do they buy from us?
- How much did they buy last year and what was the margin?
- What other problems do they have that you think our company can solve?

Answering these questions—especially that last one—establishes their plan. You can almost quantify to the number how much additional revenue they could get from these top customers alone without even needing to go out to find new customers.

Usually I have the salesperson complete this part of the exercise, and then I workshop it as a team. When I run these sales meetings, I say, "Does anybody else have an idea for Jackie to reach her goals?"

At this point, the table often comes alive, with the group offering their opinions based on experience. Now, in addition to them understanding that their manager is there to support them, the salesperson knows that the whole team is there to help. Each salesperson owns their own accounts and goals, but the success belongs to everybody at the company.

You can't have a Grand Slam without three base hits, and support from both the manager and the team will compress the learning curve for each member of the sales team. When you create an environment where people can be present and learn from each other, all these small factors compound. When everyone is operating at their highest and best in this way, it can help you move past the point of sustainability and actually grow.

Recommitting to the Individual Performance Planner

How many times in your career has a manager said, "I'm going to take the time to really learn about you and what's important to you"?

Pretty sure you can count it on one hand, if that. Maybe you did personality tests that were meant to tell you about your style of selling or were asked to write out your ninety-day sales goals without any context or plan to achieve them.

The collaborative, holistic approach described in this chapter is probably new for most people on the team—manager and salesperson alike.

Therefore, this isn't about finishing the planner then throwing it in a drawer. It's a process of executing, stopping, recommitting, and reorienting. If we get used to updating it and using it as a reflection point every other month or once a quarter with the manager or in a team setting, it starts to be something that you prioritize as a manager, as an individual, and it continues to be a North Star reminding us what we're doing and why we're doing it. Ultimately, we want our sales team to be performing at the highest level and be well-rounded, happy, and successful—whatever that looks like for them personally.

Framework #3:
The Revenue Planner

Chapter 9:
The Revenue Planner

Unlock the Value That You Already Have

You've made it to framework three of your journey to revenue stabilization and growth. Here, you'll use intentionality to find the revenue that's right under your nose and make a plan to reach your income goals for the short, medium, and long terms. If you've skipped to this chapter from the beginning, or your organization is in need of fast revenue to stay afloat, you can go to the "Quick Wins" section right now to improve your current state within three months. If you really want this planner to be your road map to lasting change, however, I strongly recommend you eventually go back and work through the three-framework plan to revenue stabilization and growth from the beginning of the book.

Let's say that you're clear on your Sales Foundations, Sales Design, and Sales Infrastructure and that you've also worked with each of your salespeople to fill out their Individual Performance Planners. The Revenue Planner is the natural result of all the work you have done so far. It's time to mobilize to start making it count.

Freeing Trapped Revenue

I spoke with Trevor, the owner of a landscape supply company that was currently doing about $7 million in revenue. They had just acquired another company and were ready to set up formal sales and marketing programs. They were talking about working with me and wondering how building out their Revenue Equation could help them make more money.

While it's relatively easy to see how individual salespeople can feel more confident and sell better, how teams can get along better, and how your sales and marketing systems can work more efficiently, it doesn't exactly show you specific paths to generating more sales and making more money. When I say building, fixing, and refining all the individual components that make up the Revenue Equation will help you stabilize revenue and set a foundation for more predictable growth, what does that mean?

You don't really know how much revenue is in there until you're able to identify the inefficiencies and misalignments. Pinpointing where leads get lost in the funnel, where money is being spent unnecessarily on lead generation, and where salespeople need more support or a change in their approach takes some doing. You won't be able to answer the question unless you are ready to be patient, stay focused on your company's growth, and keep evolving based on the results you get.

However, there are some back-of-the-napkin ways to get a glimpse of what you might be able to gain. That's what I did when I sat down with Trevor in a series of quick-win engagement sessions.

We started by looking at the top 20 percent of his customers who were responsible for 80 percent of his revenue and the type of production capacity the company had. Our goal was to find how they might bring in another million dollars to the top line without having to spend money expanding.

"What's your big breadwinner?" I asked him.

"Well, we generated about $4 million from mulch sales last year," he said. "I think there's probably another $1 million that we could sell. We acquired another facility with the capacity to make that much without having to buy more equipment."

Without all the work on the Revenue Equation in place, how could we find some quick revenue wins that would not only get him on his way to the extra $1 million in revenue but also show enough forward momentum to justify investing in building out their sales and marketing organization?

The Next 18 Months of Revenue Improvement

First—a quick warning. If you, like Trevor, are wondering how you can generate a short-term revenue lift and you've bypassed the previous eight chapters, this next section could still help you. Keep in mind, though, if you're taking this chapter in isolation, it's not going to be as effective.

Revenue is the return you get for your sales and marketing strategy and tactics. The more efficiently you can move leads into, through, and down your sales funnel, the more revenue you generate and the higher ROI you get.

In many ways, it's simple, but that doesn't mean improvement happens overnight. Improvement comes from intentionality (and comes more quickly when you use the frameworks we've spent the last several chapters laying out). The Revenue Planner is designed to support you in designing intentional plans to generate revenue in three phases over an eighteen-month period. The three phases are organized from quick wins for immediate lift to more in-depth plans developed to achieve longer-term revenue goals.

In this section, you'll discover how to use everything you've learned and developed so far to find potential revenue you've been overlooking. I give you a guide to:

- **Quick Wins** within three months
- **Revenue Stabilization** in three to six months
- **Intentional Revenue Growth** in nine to eighteen months

Phase 1: Quick Wins—The Next 3 Months

You can generate more revenue right now. I know it. But it's going to take a shift in mindset.

The objective is to figure out where to focus your dollars, human capital, and brainpower. Most people don't even think about it that way. They're just focused on the need to go from X to Y amount of dollars in revenue and then to keep growing higher and higher until they reach their magic-wand revenue goal. They don't think about what needs to change to make their goal happen or even whether their goal makes sense. They just think they'll get there by "trying harder"…whatever that means.

It's important to give yourself a realistic view of what you're offering before you dig into your revenue goals, because otherwise you're just writing a letter to Santa—putting down whatever comes to mind no matter what your current resources are.

First, we have to agree that you offer something of value and people want it. Then, we need to look under the hood and see what we can do right now to improve your current state.

What we're really looking for at the most basic level is how we can sell more, do it with as much certainty as possible with the least amount of investment and risk, and capture the most margin.

Let me walk you through how it's done.

DEFINING YOUR BEST OFFERING

If you need a starting place to identify your offerings, go back to the offerings exercises in chapter 5.

Start by listing your offerings, the revenue each of them has generated in the past twelve to twenty-four months, and their corresponding margin. You should see some clear winners that generate revenue and have clear demand and strong margins. These offerings are what we focus on right now to generate immediate revenue lift.

Trevor's landscape company had four primary offerings: mulch, topsoil, lawn waste recycling, and landscaping materials like rock and stone. He told me there was a great margin for mulch because the raw materials were easy to come by and since they had the equipment and labor available to make it onsite. He was confident that his company had the capacity to produce 25–30 percent more mulch and believed the market was there. But how would he sell another $1 million of mulch?

Trevor admitted that they didn't have the lowest prices, and their customers did not buy all their mulch from them. What they did have was a quality product and great relationships with their customers. "That's why I created the loyalty program," he said. "The idea is that our landscaper customers clear brush from their jobs and need to recycle it and that they also need mulch for their projects. But what we have found is that many of our customers are just using our lawn waste services and not buying our mulch or at least not getting all their mulch from us."

He went on to give me a convoluted explanation of their loyalty program. Basically, the customer would bring in the lawn waste from their most recent landscaping job, and his company would weigh it and charge the customer accordingly. Then they would apply it to the customer's account, adding the amount of the lawn waste transaction to the landscaper's overall spend. But here was the kicker: this amount was added to the overall spend from dumping and mulch purchase. This combined value enabled the customer to reach higher and higher discount levels.

"So, what does the discount apply to?" I asked.

I saw the realization dawn on his face. "Lawn waste recycling or mulch," he said. I could see he knew exactly what I was going to ask next.

"But you just want them to buy the mulch, right?"

He nodded, laughing to himself as he finally saw the opportunity that had been under his nose all along. He realized he should stop incentivizing what he didn't want and start incentivizing more of what he wanted. So he put the discount only toward mulch purchases to incentivize more demand for mulch. It was a win.

HOW TO GET THERE

So, you've figured out the offering that you want to focus on to create your quick win. Now it's time to create a plan and turn this knowledge into revenue in the next three months. Consider:

How are you going to increase sales of this offering?
What improvements will help the effort?
What will you need to make it happen?
What are the challenges and risks points?
How will you measure success?

For Trevor and his landscape company, reexamining how he sold his best-selling product and finding ways to sell more of it to his current customers was his quick win. It was answering those questions that helped him realize how to redesign the loyalty program to incentivize mulch purchases and not lawn waste recycling.

Next, Trevor surveyed fifty of his best customers about what they wanted to see in a loyalty program, then applied more structure to it—and way more rewards! Members received perks like a free six-pack of Gatorade for their crew with their first purchase of the month, longer terms during slower months (to drive demand), flash sales broadcast via email and SMS, and extended hours before long holiday weekends available only to members. All these benefits were in addition to an easier-to-understand incentive program that rewarded customers with additional savings the more mulch they bought.

Trevor also ensured the program's success by gathering accurate contact details from members, building accounting solutions that would support the success of the loyalty program, and providing him with metrics that he and his Improvement Team could use to measure success.

I have always found that there are quick wins trapped in everyone's company. Maybe it's developing an upsell program to your current customers, maybe it's retooling one of your offerings to provide additional value, maybe there is a product or service bundling strategy that grows your current accounts and incentivizes more leads to close faster or at a higher overall sales price. The main thing to remember is you have solutions that provide value, and if you can figure out how to provide more value with minimal changes, you will unlock the next level of performance.

Phase 2: Revenue Stabilization—3 to 6 Months

Imagine if you could improve your close rate by 5, 10, or even 25 percent. What would this mean for your revenue? Say you have a $5,000 product, one hundred appointments per month, and currently close 25 percent of them for an average monthly revenue of $125,000. What if you could increase your close rate to 30 percent? That would increase the value of your sales by $25,000 per month, getting you to $300K over twelve months.

Imagine if you could shorten your sales cycle as well. How many more sales would your salespeople have the bandwidth to close? This is what I am talking about when I say a lot of little things can create huge wins. Find all the little steps you can take to increase your odds of success and then do them.

FOCUS AREAS THAT ADD UP TO BIG WINS

It's important that you focus on improving the efficiency of your entire sales funnel before you build out new action plans to bring in leads. Prioritize improving the performance of your funnel from the bottom up, focusing on the leads closest to buying, then on the next closest, and the next, and so forth until you improve how you acquire new leads. Increases in sales from the bottom of the funnel is the place to find the highest and fastest ROI. I organize the funnel into three stages that line up with the way we organized the sales funnel in chapter 7, with prospects often entering at the top, flowing through the middle section, and then narrowing at the bottom.

To focus on what you can improve, you need to put on your Sherlock Holmes Hat and do some investigating. You'll bring together your Improvement Team and any other members of the sales team who haven't been involved up to this point. You'll also need help from finance or IT—anyone who helps you manage your CRM or ERP. Together, you will evaluate quantitative and qualitative data for what, and who, is in each section of the funnel right at this moment.

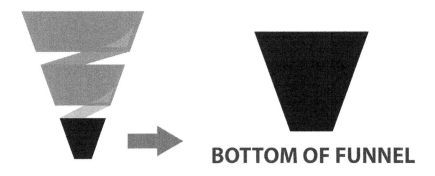

BOTTOM OF FUNNEL

This is the narrowest point in the funnel, where leads are either ready to make a purchase or are strongly considering purchasing your solution. Improvements here will yield that fastest revenue and sustainable performance, as well as scalable performance when you begin to fill your sales funnel with more leads in the coming intentional revenue growth stage.

Close Rates: Look at your close rates by salesperson, offering, and customer type. Do they vary significantly by salesperson, or are they relatively normalized? Are your close rates significantly different between offerings? Do different types of leads have different close rates (e.g., different target audience segments)?

Time in Stage or Aging Opportunities Report: Is there an average time span when most of your purchases are made from their initial appointment or from the time your team records them as an opportunity? Is there a time after which no one buys?

Last Actions Before Purchase: When you look at sales performance, do you find a relationship between success and resources or offers that your sales team might have provided?

For example, does the sales team close at a higher rate if they provide testimonials, case studies, test drives, samples, demos, or calls with current customers?

Pricing and Discounts: Is there a higher close rate at a certain sales price or discount? Perhaps you would sell more at a different price point?

Payment Terms: Is there a higher close rate or shorter time to close with certain payment terms? Maybe if you provide financing or longer terms, your sales team closes more deals or shortens the average sales cycle?

Nonstandard or Custom Solutions, Deals, or Orders: If you provide your sales team the ability to make custom deals to close sales, does this really pay off? Are they leaving money on the table or perhaps closing a higher rate because of something one of them is doing that should potentially become a standardized solution?

Middle of Funnel

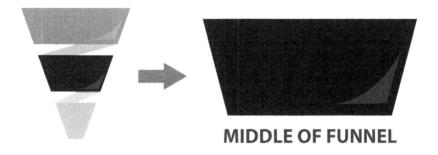

MIDDLE OF FUNNEL

In this section of the funnel, leads are considering your solution. Yours may be the only one they are considering, or they may be evaluating it against competitors (or even against doing nothing at all). This section is the bridge between marketing and sales, and if everyone doesn't know their roles and responsibilities, this is where your leads get stuck. That's why it's vital that there are well-defined, well-delegated actions to move leads from one side of the bridge to the other.

Improvements at this section of the sales funnel will accelerate leads toward the bottom of the funnel and improve the efficiency of your sales and marketing teams. You will have higher numbers of leads moving to the next phase, as well as improved returns on your marketing and sales efforts that were used to engage them to this point.

This section of the funnel is where the trapped gold lies, and if you play your cards right, it can result in some big wins for you and your team.

Populations and Segmentations: Can you find natural group-ings of leads in the middle of the funnel? Maybe it's a grouping from a specific lead source. Maybe it's a grouping based on verticals or your target audience personas. Look for patterns that tell you how the group behaves and if it performs better or worse than other groups. This provides you insights on whether your strategies and tactics to move them through and down the funnel need to be more customized.

Acceleration Levers, Sticking Points, and Deal Killers: Where do leads get stuck in the funnel? Maybe there is a step in their sales journey that has ineffective conversion points; for example, a certain population of your funnel might have lower conversion rates after you share a certain blog post or webinar. Are there certain activities that increase conversion rates? Unless you look, you won't know what you've done to open the floodgates for leads to pass through or to slam a door shut before they can get to the bottom of the funnel.

Time in Stage: This is similar to what we discussed for the bottom of the funnel, but this time we're measuring time from the middle to the bottom of the funnel. You should also judge whether there is a max time value where conversions become almost nonexistent. If there is, consider building a trigger ahead of this time horizon where you proactively attempt to change these behaviors through creating an action that puts them on a different trajectory, moving them closer to an opportunity.

Top of Funnel

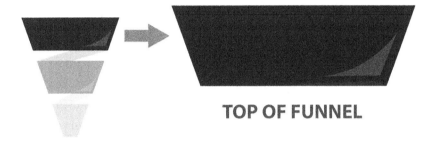

TOP OF FUNNEL

This represents the part of the funnel where leads traditionally enter to learn more about your company and your solutions. These leads have typically signed up for your newsletter, received a magnet, registered for a webinar, provided you with their information at a tradeshow or conference, or were brought into the funnel by business development efforts.

These leads are curious but not ready to be sold to. They aren't ready for your sales team to call them to talk about your solutions. This would be way too early in their sales journey and could push them away. You wouldn't propose marriage to someone you just met, right?

Acquisition Sources and Populations: Do you know all the acquisition sources for leads entering your funnel? If you do, you should also know the basic statistics associated with each acquisition source. You want to know your acquisition rates and the costs to acquire each lead from that source. If possible, you also want to be able to grade the quality of the leads from each source.

Ability to Segment or Organize: Once leads are acquired, do you put them all on the same marketing journey, with all the same content, or do you provide unique journeys based on verticals or target audience personas? Or maybe you provide a different marketing journey based on the acquisition source? Look at the data and determine if segmented and customized marketing journeys would improve performance, and thus conversion rates, to either the middle or bottom of the funnel.

Lead Actions or Activities: Do you have the ability to see basic tracking data for this population, such as email open rates and click-through rates? Having this information may provide your marketing team the ability to shortcut a lead over to the sales team for more personalized outreach. For example, a new lead that clicks on solution-related information in a newsletter multiple times or shares the newsletter may be a lead that should be escalated to the sales team.

STRONGLY CONSIDER LEAD SCORING

There's a lot to keep track of in each of those three stages of the sales funnel, and I strongly recommend you set up a way to grade each individual lead based on their actions. You didn't come this far just to start guessing how to handle your leads. This grading system is called lead scoring, and with some planning and intentionality, you can do it with all the leads in your CRM. Once you do this, you'll want to develop specific rules and standard operating procedures (SOPs) that trigger actions based on the different scores associated with each lead. This is an effective but advanced way to begin to optimize and accelerate the performance of your sales organization. If you can do it, you should.

How the Individual Performance Planner and Revenue Planner Work Together

The Individual Performance Planner poses a lot of benefits to managers. First, it helps salespeople do their best work, as I emphasized in the last chapter. It also helps managers figure out how to make projections and adjustments to plans that can maximize revenue growth.

Another thing you can do is strategize the most lucrative ways to assign leads to different members of your sales team. You make these determinations in two ways: in the one-on-one sessions where you go over the Individual Performance Planner and in your weekly sales meetings.

Based on what you know about everyone's strengths, weaknesses, and where they demonstrate the best close rates, you'll be able to play a bit of "moneyball." When you have a salesperson person who has the unique strengths to address the particular demands of a customer, you don't have to rely on a salesperson hitting a home run every time they try to close a sale. When you really know your salespeople and you've taken the time to get to know your customers, you can apply these data points to reach a critical mass of base hits. Either way, you're way more likely to win.

Take Lori and Maria at Online Academy. The two of them have totally different skills and ways of communicating. Lori is efficient, professional, and prides herself on being a concise straight shooter. Maria is a strong coach who cares about connecting with someone on a personal level. If there is a lead who has been observed to be on the verge of making a purchase and just wants to know the facts, Lori can be sent in to close the deal. If, through answers to questionnaires, the types of newsletters they've clicked through, or other data points, that person has been determined to be still unsure of how they want to move forward and is evaluating their options, Maria could help them envision what their life could be like using the company's services. It's the combination of your customer personas and your team's Individual Performance Planners that help you single out leads who are already in the funnel and maximize the chance of them choosing to buy.

Stage 3: Intentional Revenue Growth—6 to 18 Months

Every Decision Maker has a revenue goal for their company. Every single one. Whether it's realistic or a daydream, we all have a number in our heads. And that's great because when we know where we want to go, we can start to plan on how we are going to get there. This is what this chapter does—it walks you through how to chart a realistic path to a revenue target and make smart decisions about what to prioritize to get there.

WHAT ARE YOUR CURRENT GROWTH AND CLOSE RATES?

Begin by looking at the past three years of your revenue and what the rate of growth was from year to year. You might find that the growth rate will have you hitting the goal you'd projected already (awesome!). It will also help you have a better understanding of what is possible and maybe even predictable. Generally, I find that small businesses aren't taking enough steps backward to look at the internal metrics that validate whether or not their growth goals are possible.

If I were sitting across from a small-business owner who threw out a $1 million revenue goal for quarter one, I would first ask how long it takes for them to close a deal and what their close rate is. If they tell me it takes nine months to close a deal and their rate is 50 percent, I'd ask how far away quarter one was. Unless it was nine months away, and unless they had $2 million of revenue in the pipeline right now that they expected to close 50 percent of, that is not a realistic goal.

This is an example of simple, back-of-the-napkin math. That type of quick math that gives you directional insights and a quick gauge of what might be reasonable or stretch. This section goes further than the back of the napkin, but the need for a reality check is often not a bad filter as you begin this journey. So, go ahead and pick a revenue number you want to claim for the next twelve to eighteen months and use it as the North Star for the rest of this chapter.

Can You Get There from Here?

It's time to use your existing data to determine what combination of revenue-generating ideas will get you to your revenue goal. This is about understanding how you create revenue on a quantitative level. Do you know your average close rate? The average time it takes for a lead to convert to a customer? The investment amount and estimated performance of all the different strategies and tactics you and your team dream up?

It's also time to claim that revenue goal that you want to achieve, let's say, in the next twelve to eighteen months. So, do you know the number? Is it clear? Do you believe it? Does it meet the back-of-the-napkin math? That's what we are going to test the next section against. Your sales goal, and no one else's.

Let's get started with the setup and ask ourselves some questions to help chart our course.

- How is the sales funnel organized, and is there awareness of conversion rates and timing between each section? If you followed what we covered in chapter 7, you have this nailed. If you are still building out your funnel, you see the importance of well-defined steps between each stage and the corresponding KPIs.
- Do you know all the strategies and tactics you will use to achieve revenue and performance goals? You don't need to know the specifics 100 percent, but you should generally know what strategies and tactics you think will work for your business or at least be considering some strategies and tactics. This might mean hiring a business development professional; joining networking organizations; creating an upsell campaign

or a referral program; advertising; participating in promotion, sponsorships, direct mail; or cold-calling. Or it might mean a variety of inbound or digital marketing initiatives like SEO, paid search, and paid or organic social.

- How will you know if all the different strategies and tactics you are thinking of will achieve your goals? Do you have the systems and processes in place to capture and evaluate the KPIs associated with each? How will you determine success and provide attribution back to the sources of that success so that you can find places to improve and double down on your winners?

Let's Map It Out

In this section of the Revenue Planner, we are going to work together to start outlining the different strategies and tactics you might be considering to achieve that revenue goal. This is going to be based on some general B2B strategies, and not all of them will fit with your company. This is just to give you enough examples and insights to use as a model for your own outline.

You most likely have come up with some methods to bring new leads into your funnel, convert those already in it, and increase the close potential of leads already considering purchase. Hopefully you also have started to consider ways to sell more to your current customers—which is by far the fastest and easiest revenue-generating option available to most companies.

When you take the time to complete this section, you gain insights into the game plans that will get you to your goal. You will be able to make better decisions and prioritize your strategies and tactics to increase the odds of your success and decrease the risk of choosing the wrong strategies and tactics. When you get this right, your planner enables you to move from stabilized revenue on to growth resulting from a carefully designed and executed plan.

As you begin to list out all your strategies and tactics, try to match them to the different stages of your sales funnel as defined in chapter 7.

While many of your ideas may overlap different stages of the funnel, the concept of which stage they most immediately effect is super important as you forecast the sales you expect to get from each idea. This is why it's so critical to know how long your sales cycle typically lasts and what your average close rate is—so you can apply this logic to each strategy and tactic.

As an example, a strategy that is focused on the bottom of the funnel should have a much higher success rate and a shorter time to close because the sales funnel population you are targeting is already considering purchase versus just learning about you. If all your tactical energy is focused on the bottom of the funnel, any performance uptick would have a much more profound impact on immediate sales and bring you closer to your revenue goal more quickly.

The first step to start to determine if you can achieve your twelve-to-eighteen-month revenue goal is to list out all the strategies and tactics you are considering and then align them to one of three stages of the sales funnel (again, in chapter 7). This is so that you have one list of everything you think could work to reach your goals. I have provided the following example in a table to communicate the general idea (you might also find this format helpful as you process your ideas).

Strategy/ Tactic	Description	Primary Sales Funnel Stage
Business Development Hire	New employee who cold-calls potential customers, goes to networking events, and attends trade shows	Top of Funnel
LinkedIn Outreach	Using LinkedIn and Sales Navigator to build targeted lead lists and reach out to connect and begin a dialogue	Top of Funnel

Strategy/ Tactic	Description	Primary Sales Funnel Stage
Digital Marketing— Email List Growth Campaigns	Strategies and tactics to build your newsletter lists, bringing in leads you will market to	Top of Funnel
Digital Marketing— Lead Magnet Campaigns	Strategies and tactics to bring leads into the funnel you can market to via marketing automations and calls to actions to move leads to the sales teams	Top of Funnel
Digital Marketing— Webinar Campaigns	Strategies and tactics to bring leads into a group-style appointment where you can share knowledge, talk about your solutions, and prime the leads to learn more by booking appointments with your sales team	Middle of Funnel
Digital Marketing— Paid Search Campaigns	Strategies and tactics that target leads who are searching to keywords related to your company or your solutions	Middle of Funnel
Direct Mail— Special Offers	Strategies and tactics that deliver your message to a target audience who typically is interested in your offerings to solicit an action with your marketing or sale team	Middle of Funnel
Outbound Campaigns	Emails and calls to specific lists of target audiences to create interest and demand	Middle of Funnel
Reactivation Campaigns	Strategies and tactics to reengage leads who are already in the top and middle of the funnel	Middle of Funnel

Strategy/ Tactic	Description	Primary Sales Funnel Stage
Promotional Campaigns	Strategies and tactics to generate demand from leads already in the funnel based on discounts or other offering promotions	Bottom of Funnel
Retention Campaigns	Strategies and tactics to prevent customers from leaving (customer churn) and increase the long-term value of current customers	Bottom of Funnel
Upsell Campaigns	Strategies and tactics to increase revenue by selling current customers additional solutions	Bottom of Funnel

Now that you have generated your list, it's time to put some forecasts to each of the ideas you listed. This is where having historic KPIs will provide more clarity, decrease risk, and increase the confidence of your revenue planning.

You might be tempted to just write a quick check for a Facebook ad campaign and fill up the top of the funnel but try and resist that urge. Remember: tactics that affect the bottom of the sales funnel typically generate the fastest and highest ROI. Getting leads isn't the same as closing them.

Ahead of this analysis, it is important that you have historic data or informed forecasts to determine if you can achieve your twelve-to-eighteen-month revenue goal. It will also help you figure out which tactic you should choose to work with first. Evaluate the following:

- Average sales price for your solution
- Lead-to-opportunity conversion rates

- Opportunity-to-closed-sales conversion rates
- Timing from new lead to opportunity
- Timing from opportunity to closed sales
- Lifetime value of customers

Once you know these values, it's time to review each strategy and tactic that you listed in your table so that you can analyze them independently and then as a group. For each, you are looking to answer these three questions:

1. How much will it cost?
2. What are the forecasted results?
3. Do we have all the needed resources?

I now review three of the sample strategies and tactics I listed earlier in this chapter to demonstrate this modeling. Ahead of this, we need the following baseline metrics:

- Average Sale Price: $5,000
- Time from Lead to Opportunity: 45 days
- Lead-to-Opportunity Conversion Rate: 5%
- Time from Opportunity to Close: 15 days
- Opportunity Close Rate: 25%
- Customer Retention Lifetime: 3 years
- Lifetime Value: $20K

Now let's start to evaluate each strategy and tactic in the same order we outlined them in the table above, starting at the top of the funnel.

LINKEDIN OUTREACH

This is where people use LinkedIn to find new customers, using a specific market sector to search. Let's say Online Academy searches for vice presidents of sales at B2B companies that have fifty to two hundred employees. Over a twelve-month period, they might reach out to ten thousand profiles and spend $45,000 targeting them between hard costs and paying a sales development representative to contact them. If we make a projection that we can bring 5 percent of these individuals into the sales funnel, then that is five hundred leads. If our conversion rate from lead to opportunity is 5 percent, then we are looking at twenty-five opportunities that result from this strategy. If we have a 25 percent opportunity-to-close rate, then that is six new customers and $30,000 in revenue. With an average lifetime value of $20K per customer, we can forecast that this strategy and tactics will result in a total lifetime revenue amount of $120K.

But with forty-five days for a lead to convert to an opportunity and another fifteen days for that opportunity to convert to revenue, the soonest they might see results is sixty days. Additionally, under this model, the average cost per lead is $45,000 divided by five hundred, or $90 per lead. The annual ROI is approximately -33 percent, and the lifetime ROI is approximately 166 percent.

LinkedIn Outreach Revenue Breakdown	
Annual Campaign Cost	$45,0000
Target Audience Size	10,000 profiles
Annual Leads (5% audience)	500
Cost per Lead	$90
Lead to Opportunity Conversion	25
Closed Opportunities	6
Days from Opportunity to Close	45
Annualized Revenue	$30,000

LinkedIn Outreach Revenue Breakdown	
Annual ROI	-33%
Lifetime Revenue	$120,000
Lifetime ROI	166%

DIGITAL MARKETING—WEBINAR CAMPAIGNS

In this example, we are using paid social media in the form of advertising on Facebook to promote an informational webinar on sales trends and best practices for B2B sales teams. We are focused on the same target audience, which is vice presidents of sales at B2B companies with fifty to two hundred employees. The concept is to share trends and best practices that improve the performance of the types of sales teams these individuals run and to promote how Online Academy delivers programs that enable sales teams to put these trends and best practices into place. The advertisement promotes this key messaging with a call to action to sign up for a webinar with Online Academy.

Let's say the marketing spend is $10,000 per month and that on average we generate 250 webinar registrations per month. All 250 registrants enter the sales funnel and are subscribed to the newsletter and receive a series of marketing automations with additional resources after the webinar. If we apply the standard conversion rate from lead to opportunity of 5 percent, then we can forecast 12.5 opportunities. At a 25 percent opportunity-to-close rate, we can forecast three sales per month, or $15K in sales and $60K in lifetime revenue. Knowing that the complete sales cycle from lead to closed business is sixty days, we can forecast $150K in revenue for the immediate twelve months, or $15K per month multiplied by ten months.

Under this model, the average cost per lead is $10,000 divided by 250, or $40 per lead. And the annual ROI is approximately 50 percent, and the lifetime ROI is approximately 500 percent.

But let's think about the subtlety of this example. We are treating webinar leads with the same value and same conversion rate as leads that are prospected via LinkedIn. While this may or may not be the right assumption, what if the webinar leads enter the sales funnel not at the top of the funnel like the LinkedIn leads, but at the middle of the funnel? And what if middle-of-the-funnel leads convert to opportunities at a rate of 10 percent instead of 5 percent? What then? Doing the same math, this shift would result in 10 percent of leads converting to opportunities, or twenty-five leads instead of the 12.5 leads under the 5 percent conversion rate. If the opportunity-to-close rate remains at 25 percent, we now close six leads instead of three. Each month, we generate $30K in sales and $120K in lifetime revenue. Our annual ROI is approximately 200 percent, and lifetime ROI is approximately 1,100 percent.

Webinar Revenue Breakdown		
	With 5% Lead to Opportunity Conversion	With 10% Lead to Opportunity Conversion
Webinar Spend	$10,0000	$10,000
Registrants	250	250
Cost per Lead	$40	$40
Lead to Opportunity Conversion	12.5	25
Closed Opportunities	3	6
Days from Opportunity to Close	45	45
Annualized Revenue	$150,000	$300,000

Webinar Revenue Breakdown		
Annual ROI	50%	200%
Lifetime Revenue	$600,000	$1,200,000
Lifetime ROI	500%	1,100%

UPSELL CAMPAIGNS

This strategy is about selling additional solutions to your current customers. In our example, Online Academy has a new offering that they believe 15 percent of their current customers would purchase. The new offering has the following values:

- Average Sale Price: $2,500
- Time from Opportunity to Close: 15 Days
- Opportunity Close Rate: 15%
- New Product Lifetime: 2 years
- Lifetime Value: $5K

Online Academy has five hundred customers who will be offered the new solution at the same time. Within thirty days, the company forecasts 15 percent, or seventy-five customers, will purchase the new offering. This will result in $187,500 in additional annual revenue and $375,000 in lifetime revenue. While this campaign requires little or no resources to promote, we will use a value of $10,000 to the cost of the campaign, generating an annual ROI of approximately 1,775 percent and a lifetime ROI of approximately 3,650 percent.

Upsell Campaign Breakdown	
Sale Price	$2,500
Leads	500
Closed Opportunities	75
Days from Opportunity to Close	15 days
Annualized Revenue	$187,500
Annual ROI	1,775%
Lifetime Revenue	$375,000
Lifetime ROI	3,650%

Estimates and Execution

Now for the big finish! Once you have calculated and recorded all the revenue from all the different strategies and tactics, it's time to put it up against your twelve-to-eighteen-month revenue goal. As you do this, I recommend you prioritize each strategy and campaign by the revenue you are forecasting, its costs, your confidence level, and its association with the different stages of the sales funnel.

As you complete this exercise, you will quickly realize whether your revenue goals can be met with a combination of these programs.

The next steps are up to you (and if you haven't read the first eight chapters of this book, the next steps may start with flipping back to page one). It's time for you to take all this information, including the real numbers that represent what's possible, and even probable, to start bringing revenue in right now. If you keep it up, you can look forward to intentional and predictable revenue growth.

Conclusion: Your Next Steps

Congratulations! You are on your way to building a healthier and stronger company. Your sales will become more stable, and you will have a clear path toward intentional growth. Communication will be improved, and departments will team together at higher and higher levels, creating a stronger culture and better performance. The strategies and tactics you deploy to grow your sales will be more effective, more purpose built, and you will have higher and higher levels of ROI.

But it won't be easy. This isn't a leisurely day hike. This is a mountain trek.

While you and your team travel to new heights, you might lose your way sometimes. After all, you've made this plan on paper. You're bringing a two-dimensional plan into a three-dimensional world, and even though you can see a clear path as you look at your map, things will feel different when you're actually on the ground.

There will be easy days when your team is revved up and ready to go. On others, the energy you started with might dwindle. Sometimes those tough days turn into frustrating weeks. It might be because you're clinging to old habits. It might be because of problems outside of your control.

There will be muddy patches where you get stuck, uphill climbs where you have to change the way you've been doing something for a long time, unexpected obstacles where a resource you thought you had disappears, disagreements with the team about which fork in the road to choose.

Setbacks will happen.

But even though it's not easy, change is usually well worth it. And this journey will absolutely be worth it because, with every step, you, your team, and your company will be moving into a better state. Never forget that. Continue the journey, and you will see positive results for yourself and your company.

Remember—the best way to navigate change is to be mindful that things will be different moment to moment. You feel uncomfortable because you are moving into territory you've never experienced before. Be present and mindful of the fact that different is what you want, what you have planned for. You have intentionally architected this change to set yourself up for success, but maybe you've never seen anything like it before. That's okay.

Actually, it's not just okay. It's great!

When you feel like quitting, take a step back and ask yourself what is really going on. Do you still want the change you set out to achieve? Then remember where you want to go and recommit. As you lead, know that your teammates will be having similar growing pains, and sometimes they'll get discouraged too. Remind them of the intentional plan that they helped cocreate and lead them with confidence in where you are going, reviewing and recommitting to the journey often.

You've learned so much about how to team, communicate, and design a path to your desired state. Never stop using those skills. They will keep you, and your team, focused on the outcomes you've agreed that you want.

To Leave Your Old Habits Behind, Keep Walking

My mobile phone vibrated, and I glanced at the screen. It was Mark from United Events. It had been about three months since I had transitioned out of the role of Change Agent, but we still met a couple of times a month to talk shop, discuss how things were going, and create accountability to make sure the changes were sticking.

"It's Rick again. He just came into my office and told me that he received a referral to another small hotel," Mark said. He sounded furious. "I reminded him that we agreed he could keep his current customers if he focused on the personas we all agreed to moving forward, but now he's just planning to do the same thing he's always done. What should I do?"

I told Mark to take a deep breath. He needed me to talk him off his ledge. "It's going to be okay," I said. "How are things going other than this? Can you see the change? How's the team doing?"

I could hear him relax slightly. "Actually, things are really good. The sales team and the production team are working super well together. Our weekly meetings are high value, and the team shows up ready to go. Our sales funnel is getting better all the time, and everyone on the sales team is working their individual plans."

"So, what's really frustrating you?" I asked. "Is it really Rick?"

He sighed. "One of my long-term customers ended up going with another production company instead of us, and I was really counting on that revenue and wanted to do their event."

"You are probably not going to like my next question. Was this customer you lost a good fit for United Events?"

"Dammit, Karl!" Mark laughed.

He went on to acknowledge that this customer never really was that great of a fit. United Events never had the budget they needed to deliver the outcomes the customer wanted for their event, but because Mark was the owner, he would make it happen anyway year after year. This year he had a conversation with the customer, who had become a friend, and explained how their proposal for this year would cost about 15 percent more than the previous years; to keep the quality of the event, they would need to raise the pricing. The two talked through their options, and both agreed that for this year, the customer would try another company, see how things went, and then talk again after the event.

"It sounds like you made the right call with this customer," I assured him. "I'm sure the top-line revenue loss is a bummer, but this was never really a profitable event. Who knows what event might take its place! Maybe there is a better customer who would love to work with you guys over the same time period."

Mark agreed.

"Now that you know this customer isn't going to use you guys this year, would you do anything different?" I asked.

Mark paused and then said, "No, I wouldn't."

"You want my advice for Rick?" I said. "Tell him the story you just told me, why you made that decision, and what good you think might come of it. Then ask him what he wants to do with the hotel referral. My guess is he will surprise you and agree not to pursue it."

A couple of days later, I got an email. I'm sure you can guess what it said. Rick chose not to go after the referral. It was his decision, not Mark's.

The reason why?

Rick confidently told Mark, "These small hotels aren't a fit for us. They just don't make sense; they aren't our target audience, and they don't fit with the value of United Events."

Sometimes the habits you want to leave behind will catch up to you and try to hold you back. Use this as an opportunity to recommit to your path and invite your team to do it with you. Eventually, those old habits won't be able to keep up with you.

Navigating Obstacles Outside Your Frameworks

Often the challenges to our companies come from within, when we refuse to leave our comfort zones. However, sometimes they show up as circumstances we have no control over. The COVID-19 pandemic is a perfect example.

During the pandemic, I worked through the Three Frameworks with some companies who grew. They were fortunate enough to have offerings that weren't impacted by any shutdowns or a shrinking customer base and had stable enough revenue to hire more people and implement new sales strategies. The journeys they found themselves on still required hard work, leadership, teaming, smart pivots, and intentionality, but they weren't harmed by the major changes in the world around them.

Other companies, however, found themselves in very difficult situations. The companies that were hit hard by COVID had to really commit to change as they worked through their Three Frameworks and continued to prioritize building a strong company for when life went back to normal again. One company had to lay off about 60 percent of their workforce to ensure the company could continue to operate. Their resolve to ensure the company would come through all of this stronger was impressive and inspirational, but it wasn't without its stumbling points.

Blue Sky Gourmet Catering had a vision—to build a stronger company with a more diverse customer base. This would require finding new ways to grow revenue outside their referral and partner network and sell directly to the corporate market.

When COVID hit, we were about 50 percent of the way through the Revenue Equation work. Their Sales Foundations and Sales Design had been completed, and we were starting to work through how we'd design the sales funnel through exercises found in chapter 7. Then they faced not only a drastic decrease in employees but also a complete shift in their market. The work we did around Sales Foundations and Sales Design had to be modified to fit the changing conditions. While most of the work was still accurate, not changing would not only be inappropriate but risky.

As any of us can imagine, the stress for Blue Sky was significant, and when we started to create strategies and tactics to increase revenue, it manifested more and more. Their business had always been built from referrals and partnerships, and now we were going to have to become much more aggressive about sales. This meant reaching out to potential customers and bringing their story to them rather than relying on inbound marketing.

The Decision Makers were now on the front lines and had to adapt and evolve. While they realized they needed to reach out to potential customers, they were uncomfortable about what they were going to say and how they were going to say it.

Blue Sky was faced with a stark decision: finish the journey they started no matter what or walk away from it all. As far as the team was concerned, the latter was not an option, so they decided to get clear on what was important to them, to recommit to improvement and change, and to evolve.

While this represents an extreme case, it also brings into focus the importance of identifying where you are and where you want to go, then choosing to continue toward a better state. Your frameworks will help, even if they need to shift. When you face an unexpected obstacle, it will be easier to work with a plan that already exists than to try to come up with something completely new on the spot.

Envision Your Journey—and Your Future State

When you're moving toward a desired outcome, it helps to have a model. Seeing someone like you working through the Three Frameworks described in this book can help you see yourself in their position. It can help you project yourself into a place where you, like them, are seeing their plan laid out and all the good it can do for them, their team, and their company as a whole.

Holding that vision of yourself at the top of the mountain will do wonders for you, especially in those moments where you're slogging through the mud, unable to see the summit. So, I'm going to plot out the actions I recommended to a founder who was building his sales organization almost from scratch.

Dallas-based Software Development Services made $7 million a year in revenue. The founder started the company twelve years ago and was still responsible for the majority of the sales and key account management. In our first conversation, he was very clear on his goals:

1. Stabilize sales and grow review to $20 million in five years.
2. Develop a high-performing sales organization.
3. Move himself out of the sales role and replace himself with a sales team.

So, how would I recommend the company reach these goals? You already know the component parts, but here it is mapped out in real time.

I told the founder that first we needed to define the team. Based on his company size and the fact that he had not built a formal sales and marketing organization, the team was going to have to be augmented by outside experts and a digital marketing partner to generate new leads and opportunities. He would have the role of Decision Maker, and his business partner would take the role of Change Agent, with coaching and support from me. The Change Agent would serve as the hub of this model, with the required teammates the spokes.

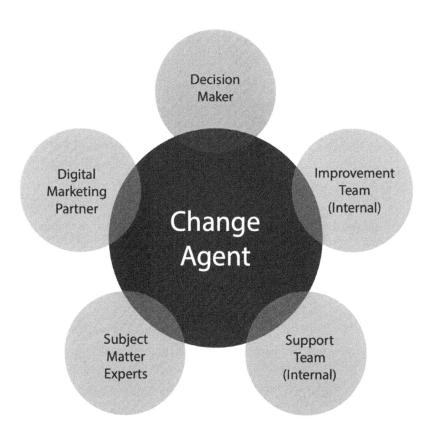

Next, I told the founder that we would need to do two things simultaneously to help begin his company's journey to revenue and ultimately intentional growth: we would get going on the first framework, the Revenue Equation, and we'd get a few quick wins like the ones described in chapter 9.

First 6 Months

1. **Revenue Equation Development:** Define the Revenue Equation Factors—Sales Foundations, Sales Design, and Sales Infrastructure—following the guidance in chapters 5, 6, and 7. Use this process of collaboration to bring the team together and start setting the company up for improved sales performance.

2. **Quick Revenue Wins:** Get intentional about increasing revenue in the short term through focus on current customers and leads in the bottom of the sales funnel. Review each customer and past proposals to find new opportunities.

3. **Messaging and Positioning Improvements:** Revise the marketing messaging to align to what becomes defined in Sales Foundations and Sales Design to improve how leads see the company. This will align the company's value, differentiators, and offerings to the needs and wants of the specific target audiences. Take the revised messaging and implement this in all marketing channels (e.g., website, social media, collateral, proposals, etc.).

4. **Preparation for Inbound Marketing Success:** Use the factors of the Revenue Equation to inform the strategy and tactics for inbound marketing. Share the information with the Digital Marketing Partner to decrease their learning curve, better align them with the company, and accelerate their success generating leads and opportunities.

5. **Sales Funnel Management:** Implement a new CRM and map it to how the sales funnel is organized in the Sales

Infrastructure outlined in chapter 7. Run integrated weekly meetings with the sales and marketing teams to begin to build a high-performing team.

6-12 Months

1. **Revenue Planner Version 1:** Develop the first version of the Revenue Planner and focus on revenue stabilization, then begin to implement the prioritized strategies and tactics to achieve revenue goals. Share this with the digital marketing partner to help them determine the strategies and tactics they think will be most successful.

2. **Successful Strategies and Inbound Marketing Campaigns:** Continue to implement and improve the quick win strategies used in the first six months and begin the first inbound marketing campaigns. Evaluate the performance of both and make informed pivots to improve results.

3. **Individual Performance Planner:** Complete the planner for each sales and marketing team member. Meet with each individual monthly to review their progress and create accountability.

4. **Recruitment, Hiring, and Onboarding of Sales Team:** Work with the Improvement Team to architect your ideal sales organization design with clear roles and responsibilities. Build a team to recruit, hire, and onboard new sales team members. Use all of the Three Frameworks to train and onboard each new team member.

5. **Founder's Transition Out of Sales:** Develop and implement a plan where the founder takes the role of player and coach. They will trailblaze the sales activities aligned to the leads generated through the Inbound Marketing Campaigns, proving out each step as defined in the Sales Infrastructure plan. Once successful, coach the new salespeople to replicate activities and performance.

12–18 Months

1. **Revenue Growth Acceleration:** Transition from revenue stabilization to intentional growth. Continue to replicate successes and use data to improve the success of current strategies and tactics.

2. **Revenue Planner Version 2:** Update the Revenue Planner with new ideas, data, and experiences from prior strategies and tactics. Keep prioritizing and making informed pivots to achieve revenue goals.

3. **Additional Inbound Marketing Campaigns:** Continue to evolve and improve lead generation through inbound marketing campaigns, using quantitative and qualitative data to inform direction.

4. **Additions to Sales Team:** Based on ideal sales organization design and sales growth, make additions to the sales team. Follow the same process as the prior period.

5. **Completion of the Founder's Transition from Sales Completely:** Continue the player/coach model until the sales team is self-sufficient and routinely closing new opportunities without the support of the founder. Ensure a successful transition with clear roles, responsibilities, and accountability points.

Get on Your Way

Believe you are going to be successful in improving your company and building a high-performing sales organization. Believe that everything you want is going to happen. You'll achieve your sales goals; develop strong revenue growth; use successful, predictable, and intentional strategies and tactics; complete integration between sales and marketing; and build a knowledgeable and high-performing team and a healthy culture.

See yourself in that reality.

What would this person, you in this ideal state, tell you in your current state? What advice would you give yourself? To your team? And what would you tell yourself, and them, when they're in the thick of the journey mapped out here?

Maybe you will tell yourself to put resources and time to the Three Frameworks. Maybe you will tell yourself to make sure you have the best Change Agent you can possibly get to help you navigate the course. Maybe you will tell yourself to really empower your team and bring all of their strengths together. Or maybe you will simply tell yourself to be patient, to be intentional, and to commit to working your plan.

Whatever you tell yourself, remember that you now know the way to move intentionally from where you are today to where you want to be tomorrow. You have everything you need to take your next steps.

You've already taken the first step by reading this book.

And I hope that, as you journey toward an improved sales organization, stabilized revenue, and intentional growth, you'll keep in touch and that I can be a resource for you in the future.

Acknowledgments

I'd like to start with recognizing what made this book possible—a lifetime of forging my own path in the business world and often learning the hard way. Without my education in the School of Hard Knocks, I never would have had the aha moments needed to get me to where I am today.

Thanks to Emily Einolander for seeing the heart of this book and helping me uncover it. With your help, I've been able to reach beneath the surface and focus on how the methods I teach work in the lives of real people.

Next, I want to thank my wife, Kitty, and my sons, Sam and Morgan, for their love and support and for providing numerous lessons used in this book. You've helped me see life from a human perspective rather than filtering everything through a business lens.

Thank you to my parents for instilling in me how important it is to never give up, always believe in myself, and rise to whatever challenges I face.

Major gratitude to all the clients I've worked with who have shown me how to live these frameworks. You are the validators who have proven to me that being my best, most creative self can help awesome teams and individuals win.

Special thanks to Brad Kemp, Leila Blauner, Dirk Dykson, and Vanessa Pence for providing your feedback and advice as I shaped the final content. Thanks also to Tom Stimson for inviting me to speak at your conferences and for being there to lend a listening ear and insightful voice. As a fellow consultant, your years of friendship and willingness to talk through ideas with me has been an enormous help along my journey.

I'm grateful to my Vistage Trusted Advisor Group for providing me with support, encouragement, and a sounding board when I needed it most. The safe space you've provided has given me valuable opportunities to grow.

Finally, thank you to Vistage Chair Don Myers for the perspective you've given me. You have challenged me to see things in a different way with knowledge, experience, and resources I wouldn't have found on my own and have helped me tremendously to become a better coach, consultant, and entrepreneur.

Glossary

Alignment: The condition in which two or more members of an organization understand and agree with one another on a topic or course of action.

Change Agent: The designated person who guides members of an organization through the process of stabilizing and growing revenue, supporting the entire organization as they evolve and implement the Three Frameworks.

Champion: Someone in leadership in an organization who empowers the Change Agent to do their work.

Decision Maker: Anyone at an organization who has the power to authorize or veto plans or procedures.

Improvement Team: the group within an organization who, led by the Change Agent, works through the Three Frameworks, developing and implementing plans that lead to stable and increased revenue.

Individual Performance Planner: A collection of goals, objectives, and systematic plans a salesperson creates and shares with their manager to achieve success in work and life.

Intentionality: Acting deliberately and with a knowledge that what you are doing is bringing you closer to a desired outcome.

Key Performance Indicators (KPIs): Data points that are used to evaluate the effectiveness of business development, sales, and marketing efforts.

Lead Scoring: A process of evaluating leads according to where they are in the sales funnel and how close they are to buying.

Marketing Qualified Lead (MQL): A lead who has demonstrated themselves as more likely to buy based on showing interest in and engagement with marketing materials.

Revenue Equation: A set of three factors (Sales Foundations, Sales Design, and Sales Infrastructure) that, when optimized and added together, result in revenue stabilization and growth.

Revenue Planner: A plan to achieve quick wins within three months, stabilized revenue in the following three months, and intentional revenue growth in the following twelve months (and beyond).

Sales Design: The creation of a company's ideal customer personas and their sales journeys.

Sales Foundations: What makes a company and their offering uniquely valuable to customers.

Sales Funnel: A process that leads pass through, from showing an initial interest in marketing materials, moving through the process of sales and marketing, to eventually buying a product; an organizational structure to categorize leads into different groups, or stages, with similar characteristics. The leads at the top of the funnel are the furthest away from a purchase and those at the bottom of the funnel are ready to buy.

Sales Infrastructure: Roles, responsibilities, and systems that allow sales organizations to efficiently organize leads and move them through the sales funnel.

Sales Journey: The path that a unique customer persona takes in order to move from their current state through evaluating a company's products or services to making a decision to buy.

Sales Placemat: A more advanced version of the sales funnel where each stage of the sales funnel is assigned clear owners with defined responsibilities, associated actions to move the leads from one grouping to the next, and KPIs to gain insights to improve the performance of each stage.

Sales Qualified Lead (SQL): A lead who is deemed ready for the sales team to get in contact with and close on their level of engagement with sales and marketing materials.

SMBs: An abbreviation for small- and medium-size businesses, where a business with 100 or fewer employees is considered small while a business with between 100 and 999 employees is considered medium-size.

Software as a Service (SaaS) Company: A company that delivers and licenses software that is accessed by users via a subscription model.

Karl Becker has founded and run numerous companies over the last twenty-five years and now works as a consultant who helps sales organizations reach their revenue goals through teamwork and intentionality. He loves hands-on problem solving and values the human connections he makes coaching leadership teams, being part of company transformations, and inspiring those he works with to find the best in themselves. He lives in Colorado with his wife and two sons. You can learn more about him and his work at improvingsalesperformance.com.

Made in the USA
Columbia, SC
03 April 2023

14695604R00117